What If "I Am You"? The Mysticism of the Physician-Patient Relationship:

What If "I Am You"? The Mysticism of the Physician-Patient Relationship:

THE DREAM

Roger G. Klauer, MDiv, MD

Book One
CreateSpace
June 2016

ISBN-13: 9781530906932
ISBN-10: 1530906938
Library of Congress Control Number: 2016906067
CreateSpace Indepentdent Publishing Platform
North Charleston, South Carolina

To my wife, Chrissy,
who is the embodiment of the
mysticism of hospitality and love of family.

Table of Contents

Foreword

What most plagues human beings with misery? I want to suggest our troubles are always some version of civil war, whether it be between nations, ethnic groups, religious groups, political groups, or just family and friends. We are quick to claim of the "other" that I-am-not-you. Divorce is not what makes us flourish, and we are all too quick to announce, "Am I my brother's keeper?" even if we know deep down in our hearts that we are just that involved with each other. From that mind-set, which besets humanity at every turn, when cooperation would be so much better for all concerned; it is only a small step to "and Cain slew his brother, Abel." Nonetheless, deep down we know we remain brothers and sisters. We are often willing to give of ourselves to excess and even to risk our lives to rescue or to help someone we hardly know or do not know at all. Empathy and compassion define the depth of our humanity. We are kin; we are kindred. The neighbor, whom I am to love as myself, is my kind. I find it a compelling and joyful happiness to be kind to my kin, whoever they are and wherever they are. It is how we are created to be, provided we do not become buried in the propaganda around us that seeks to sell us competition, friction, and violence as the only way to build happiness and safety.

Long ago, Saint Francis of Assisi discovered that renouncing the pursuit of material riches, which by their nature can exclude others from the same benefits, was himself to be impoverished. More was less. The best things in life, from the stars to the grass and everything in between, were already ours together and for free. We were rich with the bounty of God's plenty in this beautiful world. Our sharing of all of it was not to take out but to invite in the joy that is doubled by being shared with others. Brother wolf and the birds who ate out of the hand of Francis, as well as all the people he embraced, knew that he was kindred and that he treasured them. The more

Francis identified with everything and everyone, the more his life was broadened and enriched. He was poor in material terms yet rich in spiritual awareness that could be shared without the slightest diminishment. We have only to let go of our tight-fisted grasp on the societal persuasion that I-am-not-you.

Dr. Klauer introduces a way of thinking about our bond together that claims an unaccustomed vision. We need not expect to be readily persuaded that "I Am You." You may want to parse such a claim with recognition of the obvious awareness that we have different bodies and different experiences. Nonetheless, if you read on, you will be astonished at the discovery of something about human beings in their lives together that you already know—and always knew—but never much, if at all, thought about. "Mine" comes to our lips so much quicker than "ours"; "me" is so much more comfortable than "we." Perhaps we never much thought in depth about "love your neighbor as yourself."

The present volume is the first in a series of four small volumes that explore the claim that "I Am You." Do not expect an easy read, but give your mind and heart a chance to become acclimated. We are going to go on a long journey, but in a real way, you are already at our destination. We human beings are already united, and our task is not so much to make that unity happen as to recognize its presence in a genuine and fruitful way that will transform our lives together. We have no need of envy. Such thinking is the manifestation of a blindly accepted I-am-not-you mind-set. We are victims of a long-held persuasion that what is yours cannot also be mine at the level that counts most. Consequently, I need you to help me see that "what the ego desires, the soul already has," and you need me to do the same for you. In a real sense, reading this first volume in a series will allow one to add to what is being said next. If "I Am You," then we are writing these books in some way along with Dr. Klauer. Such a way of reading and of listening is surely a long journey, but the way up the mountain is always simple. One foot in front of the other, page by page, will bring you to the desired insight. If we walk together with the idea that "I Am You," we will become aware in each volume how far we have come to recognizing a truth about ourselves as human beings that is hidden in plain sight, waiting only for our conscious claiming of what we unconsciously have known throughout our lives.

—Nicholas Ayo, CSC

Acknowledgments

was raised by a mystically attentive stay-at-home mother and an intuitively wise father whose presence was always home, although he worked hard at his solo dental practice. My relationships with my wife and our five children are the most secure and reassuring influence in my life. I have two creative and imaginative sisters. I am thankful for my family's influence as a fulfilling, ever-present grace.

My wife, Chrissy, has witnessed my preoccupation with the idea that "I Am You" ever since the morning after my elaborate science fiction dream. Chrissy and our five children have seen the phrase "I Am You" subtly tagging personal items in the semiprivate corners of my life since 1991. That provocative personal graffiti has led to fewer conversations than I anticipated. As I gained confidence communicating this idea, I have shared it with some patients. I suggested the stress and tension within their private relationships and health care issues might be more amenable to healing peace from an "I Am You" perspective. I am grateful for their challenges and influence.

I want to thank Dr. Daniel Kolak. He was the first person to propose that I write about open individualism. In his first correspondence, he pointedly said it would be "nonsense" for me dismiss his suggestion. Chrissy and our good friends Tim and Mary Noble were my first editors, and then Father Nicholas Ayo, CSC. I am grateful for their input. CreateSpace provided the professional edit, interior format, custom cover, and know-how to bring these thoughts to publication. I want to acknowledge my publishing consultant from CreateSpace, Timothy Male. Tim's tone and demeanor were friendly and willing. His replies were prompt and his directions clear.

If there is any truth in the proposal that "I Am You," then you must conclude that I did not write this book alone. I have "You" to thank. I could acknowledge some of the "other" personalities in my life, either as he or she crossed my path chronologically or in the order of their importance. Their order of significance shifts each time I reflect upon him or her individually. I do not know all of you who have contributed to my efforts to be a good son, sibling, husband, father, physician, friend, and author. My introversion and sense of social decorum are a paralysis stonewalling my desire to meet and enthusiastically thank each of you.

In summary I acknowledge that "You" have taught me that we are good. We take joy in being kind. Unfortunately our kindness is brutally frustrated by the confusion cast upon the scripts of our life by our freedom to believe that I-am-not-you. Our freedom offers us the noble choice to recognize that "I Am You," or ignore that fact. I belief that Love binds us together in a massive molecule of life. Love is life's starting point. The Creator's bond through love is a valid romantic sentiment. "I Am You" is the Logos, and love utterance of the Creator fleshing us forth with all of creation, never separated from yet somehow transcended by the Creator. "I Am You" is a phrase commanding and ordering our relationships into existence. And so I have God to thank. This series of books is only a fragment of my prayer acknowledging the Logos and the permeating excessiveness of the Creator's word continuously made flesh. This is my first attempt writing a public declaration of gratitude and affirmation for the presence of God transcending and including everything seen and unseen. My awareness of my existence is many things, not the least of which is the capacity to say that I know that "I Am," and I have "You" to acknowledge for that.

Introduction: "I Am You"

A human being is a part of the whole, called by us "Universe," a part limited in time and space. He [sic] experiences himself, his thoughts and feelings as something separated from the rest, a kind of optical delusion of his consciousness. This delusion is a kind of prison for us, restricting us to our personal desires and to affection for a few persons nearest to us. Our task must be to free ourselves from this prison by widening our circle of compassion to embrace all living creatures and the whole of nature in its beauty. Nobody is able to achieve this completely, but the striving for such achievement is in itself a part of the liberation and a foundation for inner security.
—ALBERT EINSTEIN (1879–1955)

The Question: Is Your Identity Separated from the Identity of Others?

In the quote above, Einstein is saying that there is more to life than meets the eye. In addition I am suggesting that the "more" of life holds healing and peace. Do you agree that there is more to life than meets the eye? Do you recognize that something is keeping out the "more" in life? Are peace and health important to you? Einstein is inviting you to widen your circle of compassion as an antidote to this delusional prison. He offers peace through the embrace of life and beauty. Do you think you are interested? Would you like to experience more peace, "liberation," and "inner security"? If your answer to each question is yes, then let me suggest that your first step toward having more in life is to take your certainty that your identity is "separated from the rest," and consider the following.

What if "I Am You"? I know. It is an odd suggestion. It is confusing. It is radical. It goes against the cultural grain. I am not making an egocentric suggestion. I am not asking you to consider becoming me. I am not saying that I am somehow the mysterious sole proprietor of your individual nature. I am not asking that you consider inviting me to become you. I am suggesting that despite all apparent evidence to the contrary, "I Am" in fact already "You." And in addition you could look at me and say the same thing: "I Am You." If you do consider the possibility that "I Am You," then I am proposing further that this is an avenue to health and peace.

I have placed "I Am You" in quotation marks and capital letters for a variety of reasons. It is a phrase that I first came to understand when it was spoken to me, and as an utterance, it remains in quotation marks. That event will be explained if you continue to read. Second, it is a singular concept. I could have represented that fact as I have with the concept I-am-not-you, but I chose to use quotation marks. The third and final reason, for now, is that I have capitalized the phrase because I consider it the proper name for an experience of our identity.

I am not proposing a metaphorical consideration. I am suggesting that you consider the actual possibility that "I Am,"—as I have already said and will no doubt repeat over and again, in spite of all indications to the contrary—"You" and not separated from "You." Let's look at the contrary consideration. When you look at me, your standard belief is that I-am-not-you. Are you absolutely certain that I-am-not-you? What if you could be convinced that "I Am You"? Let the word "if" allow you to tinker with this idea. You don't need to fully commit. Allow yourself to test drive this thought. It was after I dreamed of such a test drive that I came to believe that "I Am You." Suspend your disbelief for just a moment. Think about it.

If you continue to read, you will be guided through this unorthodox consideration. In the end, I propose that this idea exposes a powerful pathway to health. This concept uncovers the presence of peace already embedded in your identity. The fact that "I Am You" also reveals your identity's deep connection with God, a connection that you already intuited.

How could it be that "I Am You"? If "I Am You," then wouldn't you know me, or wouldn't I know you? It's very likely that you and I have never met. Or if we have met, then you might feel more certain about the impossibility that "I Am You." Yet I would like you to seriously consider the question. What if "I Am," in fact, despite all your certainty that this cannot possibly be the case, "You"? I know this question must seem so off-putting and vague as to make you wonder if you really understand what I am asking. Trust yourself. You do understand. This obscure and seemingly unrealistic consideration is the topic of this book. I am the author, you are the reader, and we cannot even see each other. Yet in a very significant regard, we are identical, because "I Am You." Does this thought intrigue you? Perhaps it irritates you. Or is it too humorous for you to take seriously? These are normal reactions. I hope they are not so overwhelming as to prevent you from reading on.

Consider further; What if it has always been the case that "I Am You"? It is natural for you to wonder; If it has always been true that "I Am You," then how could I fail to know? Well, it was always true that the earth revolved around the sun, yet for centuries both science and the Church did not know this fact. There are, no doubt, many other truths presently functioning that have yet to be completely acknowledged. This situation is the same. Let me offer you some comfort by adding that if it has always been the case that "I Am You," then much of the world remains the same. Just as much of the world remained the same after the fact that the earth revolved around the sun became common knowledge.

Briefly put, if "I Am You," I would not do anything to hurt you. I would not do anything to hurt myself. Perhaps you have been taught that if you cheat another person, then you are only cheating your self. I learned this in elementary school. It was an early lesson on the nature of integrity and honesty. If I-am-not-you there is still an indirect trail demonstrating how cheating the other inevitably shortchanges the cheater. If "I Am You," then it is clear that when I cheat the other I have cheated my self. That explanation is crisp.

Our experience of the "other" person remains a familiar experience because "I Am You" has always been the case. But the meaning of that familiar experience of the "other" person will change. This point is important. There is comfort in the familiar although there is a change in the meaning. It is a familiar experience that the sun comes up in the morning and goes down in the evening. We now know that it is the earth that rotates, and the sun does not actually come up or go down. The experience remains familiar although the explanation has changed. The "other" person will no longer represent someone apart from you, although you will still have the experience of the "other" person. It is my belief that interpersonal relationships governed by this new understanding have a better chance for health and peace than believing that I-am-not-you.

The opposite is true of course. Trying to prove that I-am-not-you requires a fight for your right to retain separation. If "I Am You" and our connection is a given, then proving that I-am-not-you requires violent attempts to sever a natural bond.

The Method: Cautious, Reverent Rehearsal—Pretend with Integrity

I will introduce you to the operational reality that "I Am You" by referring to a dream and using stories from my relationships with patients. As I accompany patients through their health care issues the reality that "I Am You" shows up mysteriously. As you read cautiously and reverently pretend that "I Am You." Pretend with integrity. Admit to yourself that you are making a conscientious choice to visualize a new way of thinking. Pretending with integrity involves the work of honest self-reflection. Allow the information presented to enter your mind. Then wait. In that pause, engage the chore of battling your need for instant gratification. Rest within this battle of active patience and watch. Watch for an "intuition of understanding."[1] The intuition of understanding delivers immediate knowledge that you must cradle with your willingness to know what is being said, until reason arrives to substantiate your understanding. But recognize the sequence. First, you pause as understanding appears as a mere inkling, and second, reason arrives to elaborate upon that intuition of understanding. This is how you look around a blind spot. You suspend judgment and try out a new idea. You have nothing to fear by allowing yourself to experiment with the countercultural consideration that "I Am You." If what is written here is not true, then you will never lose your former way of thinking. If what is written here is true, then it has always been true and you have already arrived.

Be patient. But be warned.

"All truth passes through three stages. First, it is ridiculed. Second, it is violently opposed. Third, it is accepted as being self-evident" (Arthur Schopenhauer, German philosopher, 1788–1860). You are setting out to rehearse a nontraditional way of thought. You will face serious doubt in this endeavor as you move down the road to what should become obvious. I ask you to allow your certainty that I-am-not-you to be suspended. If what is presented here contains a new perspective on the truth of your identity, then your experience while reading your way to that insight will involve ridicule, self-doubt or rejection, and ultimately peaceful, healing acceptance.

Why would anyone read a book if the idea it proposes invites ridicule or rejection?

You face ridicule and rejection because they are worth facing if you have been tricked into overlooking the peace that is always already at home in your identity.[2] Peace is yours. Peace is the outcome. This book stirs up your former notion of identity but will not change who you already are. This book offers you an opportunity to understand more about who you are. The very nature of your identity offers peace if you stop to realize the self-inflicted violence you perpetrate by insisting in the falsehood that I-am-not-you. The "other" person, as you have known him or her, does not exist. That is the first intellectual hurdle of this book. The "other" person is not apart from you.

I begin with some preliminary guidance in the first chapter. In the second chapter I begin to present the story of how I encountered this peculiar idea regarding personal identity. As that story unfolds, I inject vignettes from my medical practice to help explain aspects of the reality that "I Am You." In the past—or should I say, once upon a time—I believed that I was one person, and you were the "other" person. Then I had a dream. My dream does not constitute proof that "I Am You." But the dream did grant me an experience that immediately galvanized me to the certainty that "I Am You." The dream struck such a powerful chord in my heart that I began to see the evidence everywhere. I did not always like the experiences that accompanied this insight, and neither will you. Therefore, be warned again: this book is not for the timid. That being said, you should also know that if what is said here is already the truth, then you have already survived and have little to fear.

I would like you to be familiar with my context as the author of this book. I am a husband of thirty-six years, a father, and a grandfather. I continue to practice medicine. I am a Roman Catholic. As a clinical physician, I break a cardinal rule of science by using anecdotal stories as evidence to support my contention that "I Am You."[3] Stories are a vehicle for exposing you to more of truth's intricacies. The fullest extent of life is only alluded to by our experience of objective reality. Stories flush out more of life's delightful details. The anecdotes presented in this book are to persuade you to consider the truth that "I Am You" is already operational, and your belief in this truth will change the world for the better. This already operational reality is why things in your life will remain familiar—albeit perhaps not quite the same. The names of the patients are not their original names. However, I have preserved Haley's name as she has already published her story and she was not a patient.[4] I have also retained Julie's name with her permission. I have done my best to protect the privacy of my patients. I respect all that they have taught me, and continue to teach.

The Tension: "I Am You" versus the Basic Meme of Identity

A primary purpose for this introduction is to point directly at the tension. Our social operations—and, I believe, the major source of human conflicts—are based upon the belief that I-am-not-you. I am saying that the absence of peace is directly related to the belief that I-am-not-you. You believe that the "other" person can suffer or be marginalized, and it does not need to bother you because I-am-not-you. But you know that the global indifference generated by your insistence that I-am-not-you does affect you. The contentions in this book antagonize the standard claim that I-am-not-you by suggesting the complete opposite.

The basic meme of our identity is that I-am-not-you. Humanity's belief in the fact that I-am-not-you is a belief that is passed from one generation to the next without question or inspection like a genetic fait accompli. The belief that I-am-not-you lets us off the hook and it absolves us from any responsibility for the atrocities of social injustice. It is not my fault or my concern that you are poor, starving, or lack shelter. If "I Am You," then I cannot escape from my responsibility for you.

Let me describe your present understanding of identity. You claim to have an identity. You claim that your identity has a location. You claim to know that the home of your identity—your sense of "I-ness," your "I-hood," or the "I-Witness" of the life you lead and claim as your own—is situated somewhere.[5] The world's scholars are not clear on where your identity is located. The world's scholars do not know the location of your claim on consciousness. However, there is one thing that the world seems absolutely certain about, committed to, and universally agreed upon when situating the location of your identity: the world seems convinced that your identity, if it is anywhere at all, is not in the "other" person. You have never doubted or questioned the assumption that I-am-not-you. This is the closed view of personal identity.[6] The tension of this book is that I, on the other hand, agree with the scholarly minority who propose the contrary: "I Am You." Theirs is the open view of personal identity.[7] This proposal is a radical, countercultural perspective on the nature of our identity, and if you read on, you will be introduced to this important avenue to health and peace.

If you have followed what has been said this far, then you know that this truth, "I Am You," must mean that you are joined with me in ways far beyond the mere writing of this book. If "I Am You," then I alone could not and do not claim to hold the entire perfected understanding of this truth. As you read, you will need to make the course corrections necessary to help society safely navigate this awareness. Einstein claimed your task was to widen your circle of compassion to free yourself from the delusion of your separation from the universe. You will widen the reach of your compassion if you begin to understand that "I Am You." You will shatter the delusion of separation if you come to understand that "I Am You." You cannot do this alone. This belief means that we are all in this together. We are a part of the "more" to life than meets the eye, and this is the essence of the "inner security" to which Einstein is referring. You have to call upon your professional skill sets and sincerely examine what you read. I am just one of the imperfect expounders of this revelation. It is a terrible revelation because of its tendency to thrust us out of our comfort zones. If "I Am You," then saint and sinner, friend and foe, neighbor and enemy are deeply related, and in at least one very significant regard, We are identical.

CHAPTER 1

The Proposal and Its Mysticism

*The eye through which I see God is the same eye
through which God sees me; my eye and God's eye
are one eye, one seeing, one knowing, one love.*
—MEISTER ECKHART, SERMONS OF
MEISTER ECKHART

Conscientiousness: Mysticism

We begin this first chapter in agreement. I am the author of this book, and you are the reader. We are two separated individuals. I-am-not-you—this is an obvious fact. In the second chapter I am going to tell you the story of how my certainty about this fact was disturbed. But for now let me be clear that I did not want to change my mind. I was not searching for a mind-boggling, innovative, or new perspective on life. I did not expect to change my mind. I acquired this surprising new perspective without asking. It automatically created a difference in how I understood my role, my responsibility, and my witness of my world's violence and peace. I have come to see that my identity is not something housed in a place totally separated from you by impenetrable barriers. Instead, "I Am," in some intimate and identical way, "You."

Why is this conversion of thought important? This conversion is important because it redefines all relationships. I am a physician. I have relationships with my patients. The physician-patient relationship is one thing if I-am-not-you; it is quite another thing if "I Am You." I am writing to you about the mysticism bathing the experience of the singularity that "I Am You." The word "mysticism" refers to a hidden reality of life. Mysticism is the acquisition of awareness for a body of knowledge you have already received. The knowledge comes first and then the understanding.

Consider for a moment the process of conscientiousness. I am directing your attention to the activity of consciously applied goodwill toward another person. Conscientiousness appears; it is a behavior we can agree to engage or discard. Conscientiousness is a hidden reality of life. The mysticism of conscientiousness is the subtle and beautiful way in which it shows up in our life. Take Emily, for example. Emily was training as a family-medicine physician. She grew up as the daughter of a single mother and as an only child. As Emily grew up, she became aware that she had no experience living around men. You might say, "Well, that must have been obvious." It is not. Emily's norm was a household without men. Emily then began to wonder how she would learn to live with a man around. Emily's wondering was a form of conscientiousness. She was attentive to the relationships in her life. Emily did fall in love, and she found out how to live with her husband. It was learning by discovering. She found her way. The process of wondering about your life, trying out different behaviors, asking questions, and learning about life from those around you is the formation process of your life. Emily's conscientious wondering about life guided the formative decisions and insights of her life. Mysticism's hidden reality, in this particular situation, is that conscientiousness reached in and gripped the formation of Emily's life. Mysticism is firstly a spiritual apprehension of knowledge—in this case, conscientiousness, but as you will see, this is also true of other virtues such as empathy or compassion—that is then secondly presented to the intellect in reflection.

During her residency training, Emily would see pediatric patients accompanied by their mothers. She took on the task of calming down mothers who were distraught about their children's earaches or asthmatic coughs. At times, Emily found herself privately being critical of mothers who could not remain calm in the face of their children's mild illnesses. Some fretting mothers expressed anger. They often made demeaning comments about Emily as a member of an inadequate, incompetent medical establishment. These frightened mothers and their berating comments frequently challenged Emily's self-confidence. She felt she could never move fast enough for an impatient, anxious mother. Emily reflected upon how she found herself reacting, and that process of self-reflection is how your personality is formed. Words like "formation" and "discernment" refer to activities of conscientious reflection upon life that make up who you are as you decide what type of person you are becoming.

Internally, Emily was privately critical of and defensive toward the worried mothers of her patients. Emily felt like a phony as she tried to put on a good face and hide her reaction toward these mothers. She knew that her negative critique of their impatience and anger was wrong. She did not know precisely why it was wrong, but all the same, she was upset with her reaction. She was also upset with the often-undeserved hostility she received from these mothers. Emily felt that her negative internal criticism of these mothers was inexcusable, although she would go as far as to explain that her irritation with these mothers was a form of self-defense. Emily had to do her work. She continued to do it despite the abuse she was shown. Emily marveled at the strength of her vocational call. Her outward responses to these mothers were noble and kind, and she was astounded at her composure. Often the child was not severely ill, and the situation only required that the child's mother be patient, comforting, and allows enough time for the medication to work. Emily wondered why these mothers got so worked up about their children's minor afflictions, and she wondered how she knew that her internal criticism of these mothers was unfair.

Emily was conscious about growing up in a single-parent home without men around, and now she was conscientiously attentive to her negative critique of mothers who seemed distraught out of proportion to the conditions of their children. Then Emily had her own daughter. Even as a physician, Emily would feel her own heart ache any time her daughter was in distress. She loved her daughter. It was through the eyes of her love for her own daughter that she immediately knew those other mothers and understood their reactions. Now, after having her own child, it was as if Emily was one of those mothers. But why did Emily even care about those mothers to begin with? Yes, it seems obvious that Emily would care about those mothers, because of the effect they had upon her work and the effect becoming a mother had upon her. But if I-am-not-you, then there is no intrinsic obligation for Emily to care for those mothers. So, why did Emily care about those mothers in the first place, and how did she know her negative reaction toward them was wrong? I contend that the answer to this question feels obvious because "I Am You." Why did she care? How did Emily know that her critique was unfair? How did she keep her composure? If I-am-not-you, then Emily's professional code requires that she cares and maintains her composure. But can you see that the explanation is easier and perhaps even more obvious if "I Am You." If "I Am You," and Emily were to fail to care for those mothers, then she is failing to care for herself. Similarly, if "I Am You," and Emily were to fail to maintain her composure, then why should she expect those mothers to maintain their composure toward her?

There is a type of mysticism in this story. There is a hidden reality here that we overlook and pass off as merely normal behavior. Indeed, it might be normal behavior, but why is it normal? What is the formation process of the normal? Conscientiousness is a human attribute. Why? And is conscientiousness merely a human attribute, or is there a hidden reality to the presence of conscientiousness? If I-am-not-you, then what factors have come into play that have caused conscientiousness to become a relevant part of human virtue? Is it merely a survival instinct that caused Emily to consider the nuances of a two-parent home? Is it only a professional code that caused her to know that her negative critique of caring mothers was uncharitable? Did Emily know that what goes around comes around, which is to say that if she wanted to be treated in a friendly manner, then she had to treat others in a friendly manner? Did Emily merely understand that her survival as a physician required the simple math of giving tolerant, good care to her patients? Or are we conscientious people for deeper reasons?

I propose that the nature of Emily's conscientiousness toward the "other" person is a survival instinct that has more intriguing roots, and those roots are not nurtured by the mistaken belief that I-am-not-you. Love and conscientiousness are not merely a pragmatic bridge that crosses the gap separating you and me. The mysticism of the physician-patient relationship is not simply a skill set developed to drawn separated individuals into a therapeutic relationship. Love and conscientiousness are the energetic glue already in place and already binding us together because "I Am You." Emily fell in love. Emily fell into the bond with her husband, and through the bond of love, she found her way to live with a man. The bond is instructional, and informative, because it includes many resources if "I Am You." Emily's conscientiousness toward her patients and their mothers is intrinsic to her bond with all humanity, which is represented by the reality that "I Am You." Emily treated those mothers kindly. She did so before she was a mother herself, not because it was as if she were the distraught mother but because she was already intimately related to those distraught mothers and their children through the always already-present operational reality that "I Am You."

"Love Your Neighbor" Is a Basic Feature in the Bond of Relationships

As another example of the operational reality that "I Am You," take, for instance, the mysticism in the call to love your neighbor.[8] Loving your neighbor is an ancient summons to a mystical relationship. We are told that the call to love your neighbor is pragmatic, virtuous, and wise.

As a physician, I have come to recognize a similar reconciling, forgiving, peaceful, and loving mysticism in my healing relationship with patients. I try to be a pleasant and unintimidating physician. I try to place myself in the position of my patients. I try to understand their symptomatic complaints as if their ailments were mine. I speak with my patients, as I would like to be spoken to. I try to anticipate the compliance barriers my patients might encounter. I offer him or her strategies for overcoming their hesitancy. Every patient comes to me to reclaim his or her health. Oddly enough more patients than you might expect seem to think their health is on a shelf in my office and they merely have to show up and pick it up. Reclaiming your health is work. I try to be a friendly but firm cheerleader, job coach, schoolteacher, and salesman. But those efforts seem to come to me automatically as if love of neighbor is an automatic attribute.

I love my patients. When patients lie to me, fail to follow recommendations, face risks because they magnify or minimize their symptomatic complaints, or step knowingly into harms way out of sheer frustration with life, then my heart aches with the disappointment that comes in an unrequited loving relationship. This is the way I am supposed to behave as a physician. My sentiments resemble the spontaneous appearance of my love for my neighbor. Emily, too, deeply respected the frantic mothers of her pediatric patients. Emily's external behavior of respect was so automatic that she found herself realizing that it was wrong for her to internally criticize their handwringing, impatience, or disparaging anger. Emily had an internal conflict between her criticism and her compassion. It is a tension set up by the conflict between the social meme and the reality. If I-am-not-you, then I do not have to take this demeaning, berating behavior from these fretting mothers. If I-am-not-you, then when a patient lies to me I should just dismiss him or her and wash my hands. But I ache for my patient's failures. Emily and I feel responsibility toward our patients through an intimate connection that is less easily accounted for if I-am-not-you. I propose that the relationships of love toward our neighbors and between the physician and patient pivot on the mystical reality that "I Am You." Emily did not first realize her bond with these mothers and then lift her criticism of them. The first thing she recognized was internal dissonance. She did not like her criticism and did not understand why she could not justify her feeling. A conflict existed between her criticism (set up by the social meme that preaches I-am-not-you, and therefore I have a choice to reject the offensive behavior from these mothers) and her sense that her critique was unfair (an internal sense prompted by the fact that "I Am You," and therefore I have an intimate connection to your struggle, in this case to these fretting and insulting mothers). When Emily became a mother herself, she gained insight into a mother's fretting. As a new mother, she was now able to see her connection to "other" mothers. Emily's doubt about her negative critiques of these mothers was initially fueled by something that existed before she had her daughter. As a mother her self-critique was confirmed. I believe the initial self-aware-ness was in place as a function of the reality that "I Am You." Emily demonstrated a connection to these mothers from the start.

The mysticism of the love of one's neighbor showing up in the relationship between a physician and his or her patient is important. Perhaps the meaning of a healthy life is held in the mysterious bond of this relationship. Perhaps health is a state of contentment within relationships. The mysticism of the bond in the physician-patient relationship is revealed in the apparently automatic appearance of Emily's con-scientiousness. We are not called to love our neighbor by some external rubric. Love of neighbor as yourself is a golden rule already in place because "I Am You." You don't set out to love your neighbor as yourself. Emily found that she respected these mothers before she became a mother. If we are taught that I-am-not-you, then it requires an external rule to remind us of this preexisting condition. If you know that "I Am You," then you will see that loving your neighbor as yourself might appear automatically, if it is not extinguished by the belief that I-am-not-you.

You might argue that Emily's response is merely empathy. You are correct. In book two, *The Evidence*, I will propose that the automatic appearance of empathy is evi-dence that "I Am You." I will let it rest here with one comment. If I-am-not-you, then why would I care how you feel as a mother? Why would I place myself in the position of these women who insult and belittle my best efforts toward their children? Why don't I wash my hands of patients who fail to follow my recommendations for their recovery of health? What happens to conscientiousness if we are taught I-am-not-you, and therefore I have a right to be independent? I have a right to wash my hands of you. What happens to conscientiousness if our individuality is championed? What happens to the automatic nobility of humanity if we are brainwashed into believing that I-am-not-you, and therefore I have no obligation to care for you or your intrinsic nobility? When the belief that I-am-not-you is protected and promoted, then consci-entiousness and respect for human dignity become devalued and unappreciated until they are extinguished.

In the field of medical education, research studies have shown that empathy is reduced as a physician's education advances. We are warned by this research. We have not figured out why this happens. I propose empathy is reduced during the course of a physician's education because education refines the distortion initiated by our basic misunderstanding of identity. Lobbying for our right to proclaim that I-am-not-you is as if to say that I am an individual not obligated to care about you beyond the most basic requirements of my profession code and its core competencies. The automatic appearance of empathy is reduced when individuation is championed to the point of dissociating us from each other.

It is further argued that too much caring might be causing burnout. Newly trained professionals are warned to guard against exhaustion. Overcaring does not create burnout. The burden of dissonance between my internal automatic desire to care and the social meme dictating that I have a right not to care is the cause of burnout. If I-am-not-you, then I am alone when I care for others. If "I Am You," then when I overcare, you are there with me taking up part of the strain. Burnout is caused by the civil war between our intrinsic nature, which is "I Am You," and the way we are educated to behave, which is I-am-not-you. Individuation is a healthy process creating versatility and diversity when it is integrated by the reality that "I Am You." Individuation is destructive when it advocates dissociation from the "other" as if a medal of valor claimed by professionals who have mastered the belief that I-am-not-you. I know arrogant aloof physicians who are neither arrogant nor aloof but created a thick skin to protect him or her self from the burnout inflicted by the belief that I-am-not-you.

A bond, either between atomic particles or between people, is an energetic phenomenon. If you enhance, break, or negate a naturally occurring chemical or interpersonal bond, there are energetic consequences. Broken relationships are responsible for disturbances in peace and health. Breaking bonds requires violence. I love my wife, children, and family. I care for my friends. I care for my patients. I have concerns for my coworkers and about global issues of war, hunger, thirst, shelter, and death. I care for others. These are important relationships. If they are broken, then both our health and our peace are disturbed. My brain has a physiological relationship with my heart, which, in turn, has a relationship with my kidneys, which also interact with my intestines, and so forth. The body has relationships between its organs, and when those relationships are broken, there are issues with our health. When an organ or a cell's individuation grows to the extreme point of its dissociation from normal tissue, this is cancer.

As I write, I think of you. I want to relate to you in a meaningful manner. I never want to inadvertently show disrespect or oppress you. Why do I care about the other person? Is it because this was the way I was raised? Do I care just because that is who I am? Do I care merely because it is pragmatic? Or could it be that I care because there is a preexisting bond between us? I believe that this sentiment of respect toward the other person, either as a family member, patient, or stranger, is more than mere politeness, breeding, or coincidence. Respect for the other person is more than social conditioning or pragmatics. Or if conscientiousness is pragmatic, then there is a more mystical root to the pragmatism of conscientiousness. There is more than meets the eye in the phenomenon drawing you and me into relationships. There are hidden values and wonderfully refreshing complexities in the attractions and bonds that create our relationships. I believe that the experience of a relationship with the "other" person is defined and governed by the fact that "I Am You."

I hope that by reading about this notion of identity and relationship, you will come to see that you are "meant to be exactly where you are...as if your place in the world mattered, and the world could neither speak nor hear...without the deep well of your body resonating in the echo."[9] Think of that: "The world could neither speak nor hear...without...your body resonating in the echo." I am saying that your bond with the world and "others" in the world is such a powerful connection that you feel it conscientiously. To know that you are exactly where you are supposed to be would reflect a perfect intimacy with the world to which nothing could be added. If "I Am You," then you cannot get any closer to the "other" person. If "I Am You," then although you cannot become closer, you can come to understand more about how the "other" person completes you. The "other" person enhances your experience of existence and the fullness of your human dignity.

If you are this close to the "other" person, do you now understand the angst of loneliness forced upon you by the belief that I-am-not-you? If you are this close, then perhaps you can understand xenophobia or homophobia in a different way. We are attracted to each other. If "I Am You," then this odd attraction toward each other even exists if we come from different cultural backgrounds. Xenophobia is fear of another people or culture that is different than mine. If I find that I am oddly interested in this strange culture, then that attraction might be confusing, unpleasant, even repellant because I have been conditioned to believe I-am-not-you. An unexpected, unexplained, yet naturally occurring attraction might generate fear. We are drawn toward each other even when this unexpected personal appeal might be toward the same sex. If this natural phenomenon is deemed unnatural by social memes, then the experience can generate phobias. As a man, if I am interested in another man and cannot explain why, that can be unpalatable to my social frame of reference even if my attraction is not sexual. I might have been taught this was inappropriate and I feel the internal tension before I really understand that tension. Homophobia might be a misunderstood natural attraction that is feared because our social frame of reference explicitly excluded that attraction from the norm. This same-sex phenomenon of attraction has recently been accommodated by the terms man crush and bromance. In the past we had created alliances, clubs, dear friendships, and vowed relationships. I am saying that we have one intrinsic relationship that is more potent than these social conventions that are developed to support, explain, or on the other hand ban relationships. Every attempt to force our separation from this intrinsic bond has an energetic consequence, creates fear, generates confusion, and even ethnic wars.

We have been conditioned to believe I-am-not-you and so these attractions move toward fear rather than acceptance. You know there is more to life than meets the eye, and part of that "more" includes the attractions you have toward each other because "I Am You." If I-am-not-you, then you are being forced to negate a large component of the "more" to life. It is as if you are being told to amputate one of your own limbs, and this is a fearsome prospect. Your attempt to negate part of who you are is depressing for all of humanity, and depression is of epidemic proportions.

When the idea that "I Am You" came into my awareness, it was a new thought, a foreign idea, and, I would even say, an unwanted consideration. How do new ideas enter our awareness? Where do new perspectives come from, especially if they are unwanted and confusing? How did it first occur to humanity that the earth revolved around the sun when, for centuries, the belief was that the sun revolved around the earth? Observation is part of the process of gathering new ideas. We have to be alert to what we inadvertently observe. When radical changes in thought are entertained, how is it that our attention is captured? I originally believed that the basic unit of a relationship was established between one person and the other. I was the doctor, and the person who came to see me—my patient—was a person other than me. I am the author, and you are the reader. I formerly understood that to love my neighbor as myself involved a deep consideration of the other person. Throughout all my life, I understood that there was me, and then there was you, the other, someone quite apart from me, separate from me in every way including physically, mentally, emotionally, psychologically, and spiritually. My patients' problems were wrapped together in their spiritual, psychological, and physiological bundles. I was on the outside looking in as I tried to help. In all areas that count, we were clearly separate individuals learning how to harmoniously coexist. I believed it would require a tremendous effort of reconciliation between all disparate members of humanity if there were ever to be peace in the world. It never occurred to me that peace was already present, and the denial of this peace was causing division, tension, and disharmony.

A New Idea Experienced as the Reality That "I Am You"

How did the idea that "I Am You" break into my consciousness? The idea, and a persuasive experience of the idea, occurred to me in a dream. It was a silly dream. At this point it is important to understand that the dream deposited an insight within me that was as realistic as life. My experience in the dream was so compelling as to reveal a heretofore unrecognized and preexisting conviction that converted my thinking. I have included the dream in the next chapter because of the important experience of my interaction with the dream characters. I was the dreamer. I manufactured the characters in my dream. The interaction between the dreamer and the characters in the dream is an example of the intricate details in the reality that "I Am You." Although my dream is not proof of the reality that "I Am You," it serves as a story to introduce this concept and its experience.

Before I get to the actual dream I ask for your patience to emphasize two more points. The first point of emphasis is the fact that I had never considered the proposal that "I Am You." The second point of emphasis is that this unexpected and unconventional idea became riveted to my awareness. It shocked me, and I was never allowed to forget it. I do not want you to think the concept that "I Am You" is mere sharing, or universal fellowship. The concept involves being identical, not like someone, or similar to someone, or as if someone, or possessing someone, or even merely equal to someone. "I Am You" is an outlandish claim. My relationship with you, as the other person, can take on many forms. If I saw myself as greater than you, then there could be domination, or I might reach down to help you. If I am less than you, I might look up to and admire you, fear you, or reach up to you for help. I might consider you as my equal or my professional or intellectual peer. But in all these cases—greater than you, less than you, or equal to you, similar to you, or as if you—I-am-not-you. Even if you are my equal, that claim does not imply that we are identical. If "I Am You," then I am claiming that we are, in some significant way, identical.

My dream exposed me to a concept I became obliged to consider seriously. In the dream, I came face to face with the lifelike and converting experience that "I Am You." As I said, this proves nothing, but the experience was profoundly persuasive. I woke from the dream powerless to ignore this unwanted new perspective. I was as helpless in ignoring the fact that "I Am You" as you might be if I told you not to think about pink elephants. Don't think about pink elephants. Impossible. It's tough to avoid doing it once the image of a pink elephant is inserted in your awareness. In the same way this dream had irresistibly hijacked my thinking. It was like a melody someone else was humming, and then I took to humming it without recalling when I began to hum. The idea that "I Am You" was a contagious idea relentlessly presenting itself to my awareness for my evaluation.

Throughout all my life, I have favored peaceful relationships. I have favored common ground and agreement. At an early age, I fell in love with the feeling I had when I lost track of time while absorbed in collaborative work, play, or service to others. Do you recall losing track of time as you played? Do you recall how time flies when you are engaged in an activity that holds meaning? This is peace. It is a state in which the space between us seems to disappear. I hope you will resonate peacefully with the mystery I am about to describe. I hope you intuit a truth in the suggestion that "I Am You," even if you disagree with my explanation for this truth. After the dream I was at peace with what I knew. But I became disquieted and incessantly motivated to join "You" to expand what I could know about who "I Am." I was passionate. I was obsessed. I seemed impotent to extract from my mind the idea that "I Am You." Yet social convention disallowed this consideration and I forced myself to remain quiet. Obviously that attempt at silence has now failed.

Sharing this dream is my invitation for you to look around a blind spot that claims I-am-not-you. You are born into the belief that I-am-not-you. By that I mean you are taught from birth that you are "other" than those around you. You are taught that you are a separate individual. I-am-not-you is an unchallenged assumption about your identity that is passed from generation to generation as if by genetic transmission. I will tell you about my dream so that you can look inside of my experience and perhaps find a reason to examine your own experiences in order to challenge the validity of this meme. What if, at some subtle level, you always knew that this was true and then came to recognize the fact that you were always already operating from the reality that "I Am You"? How could that be? You know that there is more to life than meets the eye, and the reality that "I Am You" might be part of the ingredient that has always been adding more to life.

I close this chapter by referring back to the opening quote from Meister Eckhart. This time as you read, substitute the physical eye with your name of self-reference; with the "I" of your identity: "The 'I' through which I see God is the same 'I' through which God sees me; my 'I' and God's 'I' are one 'I,' one seeing, one knowing, one love." This was the conclusive experience of my dream. The witness of my life and its script was identical to the witness of another life and its script. The identity that witnesses life I call the I-Witness. If "I Am You," then what is being proposed is that the I-Witness of the life attributed to me is identical to the I-Witness of the life attributed to you.

11

CHAPTER 2

The Dream

My wife, Chrissy, eased down the creaky stairs, careful not to wake
our children. She squinted at me in the bright light of the kitchen.
"Roger, what are you doing up?" she whispered.
I was at the kitchen counter, scribbling on any paper I could find.
"I am writing down a dream I just had."
She looked at the sheets of paper around me
and smiled with forgiving amusement.
"Honey, the night hasn't been that long."
Her eyes twinkled as she turned to go back to bed. It was as if
she always already knew what I had just come to realize.
"I Am You."

Consciousness at Light Speed

n my dream, I was a scientist studying consciousness. I was particularly interested in the effects that travel at the speed of light had upon consciousness. This is the test drive I referred to in the introduction. Only in a dream could you try out driving at light speed. As far as I know, travel at the speed of light is exclusive territory for light. The speed limit for physical matter disallows a person from traveling at light speed. Prior to this dream, I cannot recall ever being interested in the effects that speed has upon consciousness. Such as it is, light speed and consciousness were the contexts of the laboratory setting in my dream.

It came to pass that I decided to become a subject in my own experimental design. I wanted to travel at the speed of light. I wanted to know what happened to my consciousness. How did I experience time? Did past and future merge? How was memory changed if time was distorted by light speed? Did I experience everything as if it became the ever-present now? Was there a change in conscious reflection upon self while moving at the speed of light? Could I move fast enough to experience the place before thought, that place where thoughts originate? In the context of my dream, none of the previous experimental subjects had remained conscious after attaining light speed. Those subjects had left the experiment disoriented and confused. Those subjects survived, but their reports were useless. I was about to become the first experimental participant to remain conscious at light speed.

The experiment ended, and the technical crew released the harness holding me in the rocket car. The rocket car had approached the speed of light while traveling down a track that was speeding in the opposite direction, also approaching the speed of light. This setup, rocket car going in one direction and the track going in the other direction, allowed me to remain in one large room yet travel at light speed. I had remained conscious.

Baited by Reasoning That Supports Both Insight and Deception

OK, the physics comprising the setting of my dream are not sound, but it was a dream. The dreamer can make up anything. But pause here for a moment. I want you to look closely at the situation. I have used my reasoning skills selectively. I have just admitted the flawed reasoning in the design of my dream. That is to say that light speed has its limits, and, as the dreamer, I do not recall interest in the effects of light speed upon consciousness. So I have used reasoning to discard the setting of my dream as fantasy. But I used the same reasoning tool to accept the concluding message of my dream: "I Am You." What criteria did I use to decide that the setting of my dream was fantasy and that the conclusion of my dream was truth? You have to agree that both scenarios seem fanciful. This is mysticism. Something or someone has helped negotiate the selection between these two unorthodox considerations. Something or someone introduced the entire concept. Both ideas, consciousness traveling at light speed and "I Am You," were foreign to me. If both are not wrong, and both the scenario and the conclusion could be wrong, then who helped me discern the truth between the two?

I also want to pause to point out that my dream was bait. If someone wanted to capture my attention so that I might recall this dream, then consciousness, light speed, rockets, and a science-fiction motif are to me like a sale at TJ Maxx or Marshalls is to my wife—irresistible. Who was baiting me? If I was baiting myself with ideas that had never occurred to me, and "I Am You," then those ideas might have come from that part of me that is "You." If I-am-not-you, then the ideas came to me from out of nowhere because those ideas were never my ideas before the dream. Is it easier to say that "I Am You," and this idea came from you because we are connected in some heretofore-unrecognized way, or is it easier to say that I-am-not-you, and the ideas come from some unknown cognitive contaminant?

I used the same reasoning tool to fabricate a dream and its conclusions. I used the same reasoning tool to discard one aspect of the dream (that is the unrealistic science of a person traveling at light speed) and accept the other (the equally unrealistic and fantastic summation that "I Am You") as truth. You will encounter subtle inconsistencies like these as you read. I am asking you to look at the paradoxes, inspect what you might consider capricious thinking, and tinker with the ideas. I would like you to temporarily suspend your judgment. Allow yourself permission to see differently for just a moment. I am not asking that you let your critical-thinking skills roll over and play dead. I am asking that you avoid outright rejection of ideas because they seem erratic or carelessly hypothetical. I want you to grapple with these considerations. If you catch the times you were baited or recognize the inconsistencies you encounter in your own thinking, then you will become more familiar with the territory that you will encounter in your own mysteries. In this case, after I woke up, I trusted my reasoning to look around a blind spot. It was as if I had been invited, commanded, coerced, or compelled to look at and around the assumption that I-am-not-you.

Let's return to the dream.

As I sat in the rocket car, I could feel the technicians' anticipation. They hurriedly removed my life-support suit as if excited children tearing gift wrap off a present. I knew what everyone knew. I had not lost consciousness. I was not confused. I was not disoriented. I then got out of the rocket car as the experimental participant, and walking up to me was the lead scientist running this experiment. That scientist was… me! It was not the same experience as looking into a mirror. It was the experience of seeing yourself and not being alarmed to recognize that you are the person you are about to greet.

Pause.

Subject (scientist) meeting subject (experimental participant) was an experience within a dream. I possessed the first-person point of view as both the experimental participant and the scientist. I saw me as I approached me, and I saw me approaching me. That much being said, let me add that the identity witnessing all that was taking place was the dream manufacturer, the dreamer, or the ultimate I-Witness. The dreamer was the ultimate first-person point of view witnessing these events, including the subjective experiences of the scientist and the experimental participant as they met. When I met Me,[10] I knew, recognized, or appreciated all that I know to be Me. I knew what it felt like to reach out my hand to greet me, and I knew what it felt like to have my hand extended to me, by me, in a greeting. It was also the experience that we were simultaneously different and identical. The I-Witness, or dream manufacturer, knew or could simultaneously hold on to everything that was different and identical between us. The dreamer held the ultimate first-person point of view, which was also situated in what I would call Me, the home of my identity, or the singular I-Witness. The dreamer—that is, the dream manufacturer—was aware of the difference between the life script of the experimental subject and the life script of the scientist. The dreamer was the I-Witness of both scripts. The dreamer was the I-Witness within both subjects. The dreamer was the I-Witness claiming this experience as mine. The I-Witness knew this was My dream.

The Nature of Intimacy

The dream continues.

Walking up to Me, as the experimental participant, came Me as the scientist running the experiment. I knew what it felt like to approach me, and I knew what it felt like to be approached by me. He (that is, I) reached out to shake my (that, too, is Me) hand, and I saw, felt, realized, knew, and recognized "in the deep well of [my] body resonating in the echo" that I was the man I was meeting.[11] We dissolved into intimacy. We were intimately familiar to each other. There was no room for betweenness. Yet the full magnitude of the experience of "other" person remained. We were separate bodies. We were wearing different clothing. He was coming toward me, and I was standing still. The scientist seemed to expect what he saw, and the experimental participant seemed dazed by the joy of an expectation fulfilled. As the scientist approached the participant, I felt totally accepted by an "other" person, and this was a bidirectional phenomenon. He accepted me with the same intensity as I found myself accepting him. I knew that he knew that We knew acceptance. I felt flawlessly welcomed, appreciated, and loved as both the scientist and the participant. I was amazed by Me, and I was loved by Me,[12] a Me that was greater than me yet still just me.

In the dream we looked identical. But who was looking? The I-Witness of this event seemed to be everywhere. Yet I knew we had extraordinarily different life paths.

I knew all of his life as if it were mine, yet I retained a complete understanding of how we were different. I knew where I got out of bed that morning before the experiment. I also knew where he, that was also me, got out of bed that morning. These were not the same places or lives. Yet we both knew everything about each other. I not only knew every life choice we had made but the motives behind each choice and the various probable outcomes. I recalled the hurdles I had overcome in my personal life to arrive at both career paths I had taken as the scientist and the experimental subject. And still there was no judgment, just overwhelming acceptance and understanding without regret. I experienced a sense of all-encompassing contentment to which nothing could be added and from which nothing was missing.

It is interesting to note that when the scientist reflected on the life of the experimental subject, neither life-script disappeared; both scripts were held within the awareness of the singular I-Witness doing the reflection. That is to say that the identity witnessing the life script or event—whether it was the scientist or the experimental subject reflecting upon his life—was able to hold familiar, as if his own, both scripts that he witnessed. That singular identity was the I-Witness of the events involving the scientist and experimental subject. Perhaps the multiple people in our lives are like multiple characters in our dreams. The dream was suggesting a reality in which the "others" and their life scripts were observed by one I-Witness.

It was because of the fact that "I Am You" that I knew both lives instantly as if the memories of both lives were mine. Nothing was lost. That is to say I did not forget who I was as I moved between the two lives. This subtle point is important. If it is already an established and operating principle within our life that "I Am You," then nothing is lost when this fundamental truth becomes the reality of our thinking and behavior. Although the scripts (the scientist's life story and experimental subject's life story) witnessed by this first-person point of view did, in fact, change, the witness—that singular identity, that I-Witness—did not change, and I did not forget who it was that witnessed the different scripts. Both lives and their stories or scripts were mine. The ultimate first-person point of view, the owner and manufacturer of this dream, clearly rested within the singular I-Witness author of this dream. The I-Witness was not the script but observed the script and claimed the script. The location of our identity (scientist and experimental participant) was intimately within the singular I-Witness. The I-Witness is not defined by or confined to the script it witnesses. The I-Witness is that thing that observes your life. The I-Witness sees the events of your life pass in front of it. The I-Witness is that thing that says, "This is my life." The I-Witness claims what it observes. The I-Witness says, "I saw this" or "This is what happened to me" or "This is familiar."

This experience can be compared to the conversation you have in your head. If you ask your conscience about right and wrong, the conversation you are having is with you. You are speaking to you. If you ask yourself a question, you might get an answer. But you know that the conversation you are having between you and your conscience is a conversation within you. You know you own it. You know the most authentic version of you is conscience. The other subjective point of view, which might be challenging conscience, is also yours, and it is not conscience yet is intimately related to conscience because both voices are in the same head, so to speak. Both of these voices are conversing with each other inside of your head, and you have manufactured those two voices. They have the same I-Witness. You might call the voice that argues with conscience a demon. But it's your demon. It is you. When you say, "Why can't I make myself stick to my diet?" the answer is because you haven't decided to go through the pain or discomfort of doing so. Sticking to my diet requires resources not confined to me alone. I need help. If "I Am You," then it takes you and your help. If "I Am You," then I also have to agree to receive your help. But who precisely does that "You" include? I want to eat, drink, and be merry. I want to lose weight. Both of those scripts—eat, drink, and be merry and lose weight—are desires witnessed by one I-Witness. When Emily criticized the anxious mothers and then labeled her criticism as unfair and wrong, both of those voices were her voices. My point is that perhaps the experience of one singular identity, or one singular I-Witness, or the experience that "I Am You" might have similar features to the experience of multiple voices in one head or the multiple characters in one dream. All the voices in my head are part of me. They are mine. All the characters in my dream are part of me. They are mine. All the people in my life are no longer apart from me if "I Am You." We are somehow intimately related.

There is one more consideration. The actions of conscience in conversation with you are witnessed by the I-Witness. The I-Witness is not confined to conscience. The I-Witness is not confined to the desires it witnesses. Why do I suspect this? Because I "blame" the I-Witness for bringing things—thoughts, incidents, insights, examples, situational perspectives—to my conscience for its consideration, its blessing, its imprimatur, or its challenge. The I-Witness sees novel scenarios from my life script that I have never considered before. Emily's I-Witness saw her critique of those fretting mothers and also saw her conscientious response to her critique. The I-Witness does not seem to be confined to conscience or the script of my life. The I-Witness sees what conscience has to say. The I-Witness sees the script of the life I claim as mine.

The scientist running the experiment and the experimental participant were simultaneously me yet not the author of the dream, and both were observed by the same I-Witness. The I-Witness was the most real yet least real thing of all because the I-Witness was not the object of any subject. The I-Witness is not witnessed. It cannot be seen. It is not the object of another subject. But without this most real part of my dream, that "unwitnessable" I-Witness, or the unobserved observer, I would know nothing about this dream. That was my experience.

Risking another distracting digression from the story of the dream, I have to point out another feature of this dream that may otherwise be overlooked. If I-am-not-you, then every time I shifted from the experimental subject to the scientist, that experience would have more likely felt as if I was reading the mind of the other person or in some way possessing him or was leaving one body and was forced to enter another body. When Roger Subject met Roger Scientist, why did I feel deep, accepting intimacy and not startling, threatened surprise? I knew what both sides were thinking. I knew I could trust both. I had accepted both. This is why my response was a loving "I Am You" and not an agitated, "Who the hell do you think you are, impersonating me?" By way of an example, if you have seen the 2003 film *Freaky Friday*, then you know that Lindsay Lohan wakes up in the body of her mother, Jamie Lee Curtis. They are shocked when they see each other in their respective bodies. In the waking world, if I am convinced that I-am-not-you, and I came upon myself, I would be shocked as if to say, "Who is stealing my body?" or "Am I who I really thought I was or someone else?" In the dream, this was not the case. I contend that it was not the case because the ground upon which the dream experience took place was designed to allow me to see around the blind spot that is I-am-not-you. The dream was designed to allow me the possibility of experiencing the reality that "I Am You." Who designed such a wonderful dream? It was me. However it was a Me that is greater than me. I suspect it was a Me that included "You." If this was true then there must be evidence.

CHAPTER 3

Mysticism Camouflaged in Familiarity

What makes his world so hard to see clearly is
not its strangeness but its usualness.
—ROBERT PIRSIG, ZEN AND THE ART OF MOTORCYCLE
MAINTENANCE: AN INQUIRY INTO VALUES

Gia Shows Compassion to Mac; Daniel Reacts to the Suffering of Hondurans

When you look for the evidence that "I Am You," one of its features is that it resonates with some part of your being. The evidence might strike a chord and harmonize with a basic truth about the foundational ground of your experience of existence. If you feel familiarity with the evidence and stories I present, then this might be an important clue and cue for the presence of truth. Familiarity is an intrinsic feature of the fact that "I Am You," and familiarity is the disguise hiding the fact that "I Am You."

Consider your empathetic reactions to this story of compassion. Can you affiliate with this next vignette? Does something in the story feel familiar to you? Is it familiar simply because it might have happened to you or because something more significant is going on? Could it be a familiar story because it represents evidence that "I Am You"?

It was a winter morning, and Mac was a one-year-old boy being shuffled out of his car seat into the stroller in the clinic parking lot. It was snowing heavily, and his mother was also trying to make sure that Mac's three-year-old sister, Gia, was standing close by and not wandering into traffic. Mac saw the thick, falling snow and opened his mouth to the sky, catching snowflakes on his tongue and face. He bobbed and shifted his head, trying to catch snow on his tongue, and then he ripped off his mittens and touched his tongue as if his tongue was not working. He felt nothing and tasted nothing. He seemed to be wondering why everything else placed in his mouth had some sensation, and this magnificent snowfall felt like nothing. He could hardly hold his eyes open in the falling snow, but that did not matter; he could not taste the snow. I stopped to help Mom organize herself in the slush before plodding into the clinic. I saw Gia laugh sympathetically at her little brother. During the commotion of exiting the car and entering the clinic, Gia was watching over Mac. She was patting her little brother on the shoulder.

"You can't feel it, Mac. You can't taste it," she said.

As she struggled to comfort Mac, Gia looked up to us as if to say, "You are grown-ups. Can't you help me to help him understand what is going on so he can stop fighting to feel and taste this snow?"

We could see Mac's struggle to feel and taste snow, and we could see Gia's struggle to give her brother some relief or explanation. Regardless of whether you can or cannot feel and taste snow, Gia saw her brother struggle, and she expected our help.

Is this a story of empathy, compassion, and sympathy? Is this the story of three-year-old Gia's conscientiousness? Are you familiar with the sensations of Mac, Gia, and those of us who saw this event unfold? Gia was three, and Mac was one. What is going on here? My contention is that if "I Am You," then it would seem a very natural consequence that I would automatically be interested in how you feel (empathy) and bend my sensitivities (sympathy) toward your hard times and self-interests with the intent to share (compassion) the burden of any suffering you might encounter. Gia knew that Mac was struggling. She was only three but perhaps recalled her own struggle to feel or taste the falling snow. But why would she be motivated to ease Mac's struggle? Why would she care about Mac's struggle? Is it sufficient enough to say that Gia cared because she had a similar experience in her short life? It might have merely been sibling love. But I contend that if "I Am You," then Gia knows something about Mac. In some significant regard, his private struggle is hers, and she is familiar with the predicament; she knows she can grant it relief. She knows she will feel better if she grants him relief. She knows it feels good to grant others relief.

We know our graciousness toward others feels good to us. Is that because if "I Am You," then serving you with my generosity or graciousness has direct impact upon me? What I am saying is that virtues such as empathy, sympathy, and compassion might be automatic behaviors because "I Am You." Why might most of us walk by and perhaps only be attentive enough to see the silly humor in Mac's struggle to taste snow? Why might most of us completely miss the fact that Gia is trying to grant her little brother relief? I want you to look closely at Gia's reaction to Mac. It is automatic behavior, regardless of the fact that most adults have already extinguished this automaticity. It is a natural peaceful behavior that I believe is extinguished by a social meme that insists that I-am-not-you. It is a meme that teaches us that those responses like Gia's are not required. Those responses are not automatic. We are taught that a response like Gia's is silly and childish. My awareness of this tiny little struggle in a parking lot could easily have been overlooked. I am a busy man. I have time constraints, commitments, and places to be, and their struggle should be inconsequential. But I did notice. I did wonder. I saw a bigger picture in this little incidence of honest brother-sister interaction. I did not stop and think about helping this mother. I did not stop and think about witnessing Gia's interaction with her brother. I saw it, and I stopped. It was automatic. Why? Perhaps no reason is needed. I am suggesting there is something extremely peaceful and precious in this automatic behavior between a sister and her brother, and that this behavior stems from the underlying reality that "I Am You." It is because of this connection that Gia was compelled to try to offer relief to her brother. In addition my contention is that our behaviors deviate from these automatic responses of empathy, sympathy, or compassion like Gia's because we have been taught that I-am-not-you.

If I-am-not-you, then I do not need to be concerned with your struggle. If I-am-not-you, then I do not see the motive for humanitarian gestures. After all, it does not feel good to share your struggle. If I join in your struggle (find solidarity in your cause), I might fail to provide relief for your struggle. I might not feel satisfaction. So why bother? Well, like it or not, we are bothered by each "other's" struggles. And if you ask people who do fall into solidarity with the struggle of others, those humanitarians will not tell you that their motive was to feel good. Their motive was they could not just stand by and watch; they were compelled to get involved. The belief that I-am-not-you does not seem to be a belief that would compel my involvement in your struggle. Humanitarians will tell you that their involvement might have been hard and required a great deal from them, but they received more than they gave. If you give or your self to a humanitarian gesture, then that implies a cost, or a reduction. But if the outcome of giving away of your self is to actually receive more than you gave, then how do you account for that math if I-am-not-you?

Our son Daniel came home from a humanitarian trip to Honduras. He was a first year dental student at the time. After I listened to all of his stories I had two pointed questions. As a freshman dental student would you be allowed to do these dental procedures on an American patient? After you do the math what is your summary conclusion? I was asking Daniel if what he gave to the people of Honduras was more or less than and what he received from the Hondurans. His answer to the first question was that he was well supervised. He got my point. He was never to learn how to do things without supervision and the advised consent of the patient no matter the country. His answer to the second question was that he received more than he gave. If I-am-not-you, and if Daniel received more than he gave, then as a young man from one of the richest countries in the world had he just robbed some of the poorest people in the world? If "I Am You" then of course he received when he gave. And if he gave well, then he received well in return.

Like it or not, Gia was bothered by Mac's struggle. Daniel was bothered by the potential implication that he had taken more from the Hondurans than he had given. Gia did not have to be taught that she was bothered. She was bothered. Daniel did not have to be taught how to recognize suffering. He was bothered. Gia does not have to be taught how to love Mac. Sibling love is the glue already in place because "I Am You." Gia might learn to hate her brother or learn to convince herself that his struggles should not affect her because I-am-not-you. Daniel did not have to be taught that he should care for the suffering of a stranger in a strange country. He cared.

I believe we have been taught that we have a choice, and we don't need to love our neighbors. We have been taught that we do not need to be bothered. But the fact is this; we are automatically bothered, and the ills of society are the result of our attempts to extinguish that automatic behavior and try to prove that we do not need to care. The only real choice we have is the choice between ignoring that "I Am You" or believing that "I Am You," but the connection with our neighbor is already established. The energetic bond is in place. Breaking that bond requires an effort that is ultimately violent. The fact is that "I Am You," and, like it or not, I am bothered by your struggle, even if I am only three years old, and you are only one year old, and your only struggle is that you cannot understand why you cannot feel or taste the snow. Is there something familiar in this story? Does the familiarity perhaps encourage you to consider the possibility that it emanates from the already-established fact that "I Am You"? That is all that is being asked. Will you pretend for a moment that "I Am You"? Do you see a difference?

Affirm, Negate, Affirm: Margaret Wanted to See the Doctor On Call

Let's continue with the dream, after I apologize for the sentence you are about to read. My wife Chrissy was my first editor. Chrissy cringed whenever she read a sentence greater than two lines. "I just stop reading," she said. Please continue to be patient. Trust yourself. You do understand.

The dream continues.

I, the subject, approached Me, the scientist. I was extremely shy and hesitant as if approaching a stranger, although simultaneously I was full of certainty, awareness, and intimacy, knowing that the one I was speaking to was in every way—regardless of every apparent contradiction and impossibility—Me, not me, yet certainly had to be Me.[13]

This feature—affirm, negate, affirm (or Me, not me, yet certainly Me)—is another street sign encountered on the road of an experience with mystery. I want you to watch for the times you find yourself in this cognitive pattern of affirming, negating, and then reaffirming something to yourself. When you affirm-negate-affirm, then be alert! Paradox, or facing the potential for the coexistence of contradictory realities, goes hand in hand with the experience of mysticism. When this signal appears, you might be approaching knowledge that is first apprehended and then understood by the intellect. Affirm-negate-affirm is honesty. When you affirm-negate-affirm, you do so with some certainty and a sense of deep familiarity. It is a version of honesty that requires your patience and versatility in thought. You will need this flexibility in order to defy convention. Affirm-negate-affirm—or I know, but I really don't know, and yet I feel I am certain that I do know—is an expression of your honesty as you look for reason to explain what you understand. Affirm, negate, affirm is a herald for the experience of the acquisition of knowledge that is about to be understood or explained by the intellect.

Let me offer another example of this precept. Margaret was a patient paralyzed on her right side from a stroke. I was on call. She was not my patient. I did not know her. I was her covering physician that early Sunday morning. I came to the rehabilitation unit, and Carol, the nurse, came to meet me.

"Margaret wants to see you," Carol said in a tone that implied I should know her.

"Who's Margaret?" I asked.

Carol handed me the patient's chart and walked me to her room. Those were the days of paper charts. It was 5:30 a.m. Margaret was wide awake, waiting to meet the doctor on call. I introduced myself to her and did an exam of her heart, lungs, and legs (looking for evidence of a blood clot, which is a complication for the paralyzed extremity of a bedridden patient). I got Margaret to move a bit. She had no complaint. She merely wanted to meet the physician on call. Carol left the room. I sat down in the patient's room to write my note. Then I got up and looked at Margaret's legs again.

I listened to her chest again. The exam was negative. She was paralyzed on the right, but aside from that, she seemed as stable as the notes from the previous day. I left the room and asked Carol to order a lung scan to look for a pulmonary embolism (PE).

A PE is a life-threatening blood clot thrown from the leg to the heart and lungs. In those days, looking for a PE would require calling technicians in on the weekend to run the test and then calling in a physician to read the test at the hospital. If you were suspicious of a life-threatening PE, then you were also obligated to initiate a risky medication until the threat was ruled out. I called for the team to come in and started the medication.

This was a big deal. Carol asked me for a reason.

"They are going to ask me why you want this test, and just saying, 'To rule out a PE' will not cut it. You need a physical finding or symptom."

I took Carol into the room with me and told her that Margaret had pleuritic chest pain. Pleuritic pain is a chest pain someone has when he or she takes in a breath of air. Carol disagreed. Margaret did not have that pain. I coached Margaret to take in such a deep breath that it would hurt anyone, and when she grimaced, I turned to Carol for her acquiescence. Carol agreed that something was wrong with Margaret. Carol agreed that her request to be the first to see the on-call physician was peculiar. Carol agreed that Margaret did not look right. But Carol disagreed with my physical finding and my near-fabrication of a patient's symptom. Carol warned me that those on call would be kicking up a fuss.

As I was leaving church later that Sunday morning, my car phone (yep, the phones were confined to cars back then) rang. I told my daughter she would have to be quiet because the people calling were probably going to yell at me for making them work on a Sunday. She looked at me sympathetically with a "Daddy, you didn't?" look in her eyes. I answered, and Dr. Ball practically shouted, "How did you know?"

I sheepishly asked what he meant.

"How did you know?" he repeated.

I answered honestly, "I didn't know."

"Damn right," he said. "I examined her before the lung scan, and she had no physical findings, yet she threw a huge PE. She has been transferred off the rehabilitation unit and into the ICU, and all is well."

I explained that she was a stroke patient and at risk, and so I was suspicious.

"It was more than that," he said. "How did you know?"

I agreed that it was more than that, but precisely what makes up the "more" is not completely clear.

I knew that Margaret had thrown a life-threatening PE, yet I certainly did not know, but I have to say, yes, I did know. Affirm, negate, affirm—that is a dicey trio, but it is a frequently encountered trio appearing in the presence of a miracle or the mystical. Margaret, Carol, and I had a therapeutic relationship. There was a bond between us. We did not know each other well, and the work we accomplished that morning was lofty and seemed to defy reason. But there is mysticism in the physician-patient relationship, which I feel can be explained because "I Am You." At least it is easier for me to explain than if I-am-not-you. If "I Am You," then there are things we can come to know about each other, although we might not be precisely sure how we came to know them.

When I asked Chrissy to marry me, I knew she would say yes, but I did not really know that, but then again I did know. When I asked her to read my manuscript I knew she would be a good editor, but then I wasn't sure I would survive her edits, but of course I have. There is mystery in the act of asking someone to spend the rest of his or her life with you. The vow's mystery is certain, doubted, but reaffirmed. That mystery is sustained in the vow until the vow is broken, and then the energy in the bond of that original mystery is broken and lost. Mysticism is in the bond of all relationships. There is energy there. If "I Am You" is true, then there is energy in what binds us together in our identical "I Am." Breaking that bond (or perhaps I should say any attempt at breaking that bond, as I am not sure if the bond making us identical can be broken—you will have to weigh in on that part of the truth) by saying, "I-am-not-you" has negative energetic consequences with both our peace and health. Chrissy probably did not read that last sentence either.

I Met Me, and I Knew That "I Am You"

The dream continued.

Once again returning to the action of the dream, I approached this version of Me in a gradual, sensitive, and guarded way. I feared that the slightest wrong move would frighten away the delicate balance of an awareness I had for the intense intimacy of the situation. I enjoyed this intimacy immensely. I knew it. It was familiar. It was uplifting. It satisfied my longing for the "more" in life. It was nostalgic. In meeting me, there was a deep sense of returning home coupled with a pang for having ever left this place of contentment. I did not want the feeling to be extinguished. So when I spoke for the second time, I did so softly, gently, and cautiously. I knew that he knew what I was about to say. Yet I did not know that he knew. Still I did know that he knew, and yet I did not want to disturb what he knew, and so I said, "'I...I Am You.'" I declared it with certainty, yet as a meekly asked question, yet truly certain of what I knew.

And I, the scientist, calmly, lovingly, nonchalantly, and with skin-penetrating kindness in tone and texture of voice, said slowly, in a hushed, receptive, reassuring whisper as if breathing into me, "I know."

Which I already knew he would say. But I did not know how wonderful it would feel to hear it.

"I know," he said, and I felt it! But I doubted. How could this be?

I needed verification. I was not absolutely sure he really understood, although we looked identical, and I knew what he knew. I (the experimental participant) self-consciously and cautiously, so as not to offend, drive off, or disturb the reality that was Me (the scientist), whom I already knew clearly understood the situation, was compelled to verify what I had just said and in some way prove that I was understood. So I risked shattering the whole experience. I risked ridicule or rejection, and I repeated my claim.

"Perhaps...perhaps you misunderstood. I'm saying 'I...Am...You.'"

And the scientist said, with his smile exceeding any sense of acceptance I had ever experienced, often imagined, and now felt with intimate familiarity, "I know. I know that 'I Am You,'" said the scientist.

In the dream's conversational sequence, I met Me, knowing all the sinful and saintly features of my history. I met Me and was met by Me with forgiving and encouraging acceptance. I had met the "I" embedded in all human dignity. I deeply accepted, understood, and forgave who I had met. I decoded that experience in the only way I could understand. It all seemed so familiar, yet I was sure this had never happened before. I had completely lost track of time. The immense joy and wonder of the unfolding of this meeting was cast in a spell of perfect contentment. I felt supremely welcomed to life's fullness. I was awe. I was the awe that grants humanity its dignity. I was not in awe. I was awe as much as sap is to tree or blood is to life or life is to life.

Had the "I-Witness" of my life and dreams just reflected upon the "I-Witness" identical to us all and with no object in between? Is that possible? Something had taken place that was familiar yet brand new and still certainly familiar. Whatever had happened, I did not want it to end. Simultaneously I knew it never ended.

I think I have a self. My intuition of self's existence was verified because I met I. Yet at the moment of writing this sentence, as profound as the experience continues to be, something greater than Me meeting Me continues to take place in a place that is not the object of the I-Witness but must be in, of, or as the I-Witness. I rested in the same place as the I-Witness. I occupied the same vantage point as the I-Witness identical to all of us.

You watch your life unfold in front of you. That thing in front of which your life unfolds is your I-Witness. The I-Witness of your life is an involuntary observer. You must watch your life. Even when you are not attentive, then you are watching your inattentiveness to life because you can say, "I missed that" and know that you missed something, even if you do not know what it is you missed. You can purposefully turn away from life, and you witness turning away. The I-Witness observes your life unfold. The I-Witness watches the script of your life. The I-Witness is not the script. The I-Witness sees the play or story of your life evolve, but the I-Witness is not that story. The I-Witness is the story's claimant or observer. That thing, your I-Witness, is your identity, and it is identical in all of us, although what it witnesses is not identical.

My experience in the dream was that the I-Witness of the life script attributed to the scientist and the I-Witness of the life script attributed to experimental subject were one identical I-Witness. It was also my experience that the I-Witness influences that which it witnesses. This is not achieved by the I-Witness reaching out and touching or manufacturing objects to become experiences. The I-Witness influences what is witnessed because the I-Witness is the foundation, ground, and platform upon which all that is witnessed appears and meets witness. I am proposing that the one identical nature of the I-Witness infects, contaminates, flavors, in some way influences, gives presence to, or allows for all that is the object of, or the script to, the I-Witness. The I-Witness is not the script that it claims as its own. But in some way I believe the I-Witness participates in the script writing. Our life scripts have virtues written into them. One might wonder if compassion, empathy, and sympathy exist as valued human attributes due to the fact that we have one identical I-Witness. In that one identical I-Witness the attributes of empathy, compassion, sympathy, conscientiousness, and conscience have been vetted and been found to be valuable. If I-am-not-you, then why would I care to share in your passions (compassion)? If I-am-not-you, then why would I care what things feel like to you (empathy) or care why a stranger hurts, struggles, or is suffering (sympathy)? If I-am-not-you, then how could I know what "You" have already determined is wise behavior (conscientiousness and conscience), and hear about that wisdom in a voice that sounds like mine?

I believe the ills of the world are because we continue to insist that I-am-not-you. It is as if I insist that I-am-not-you because it lets me off the hook. I can escape from responsibilities that seem overwhelming. If I-am-not-you, then I need not be bothered. But just like Gia and Daniel, you are bothered by the struggles of apparent "others." Margaret's situation did bother Carol and me. Emily was bothered by the absence of a man in her single-parent home and by her reaction toward conscientious mothers. You are bothered by what happens to those around you.

In my handshake with me, "Such a powerful thing passed between us at that moment, utterly ineffable, that I would only venture to say it was something primordial—a thing between two men, or one man, or none I cannot say, for we both were but dream men—yet utterly sacrosanct."[14] And I said to me, "'I Am You.'" That which passed between us was recognition of a bond. I can call it a spirited impulse, mysticism, or the apprehension of a truth that in no way could be apprehended. I always knew there was something "more" in life. Now I had experienced the "more" whose exquisiteness I had always intuited, never met, and yet must have met because it was the very definition of familiarity.

CHAPTER 4

The Physiological Impact of Empathy, Rapport, and Seeing around a Blind Spot

As a physician, the fullest expression of an empathetic rapport between patient and physician is "for an alliance to begin; the patient needs to feel heard and seen—that is, met by another person."
—HELEN RIESS, MD, AND CHRISS GORDON, MD[15]

Not without My Finger

The sensation I felt in the dream was the perfect alliance Riess and Gordon mention in the quote above regarding their research into empathy. In meeting me, there was the ultimate in empathetic rapport. I felt a deeply familiar empathy. As scientist and experimental participant, we were apart yet intimately related. I was truly met by another and knew the experience of that meeting as both the originator and receiver of a perfectly safe alliance. It was perfect interpersonal peace.

In the aftermath of this dream, I had an array of physiological reactions. Our bodies and how they function is known as the body's physiology. Our bodily reactions give us information. The information from a physical reaction can sometimes arrive in our awareness before our reasoning skills have the time to interpret the data. Our physiological reactions might reveal connections to each other before we can explain how we could have these connections. I am going to explain this effect by using a story to direct your attention to your body and its reactions to information. Your role is to see if your body reacts to the story. Read on and watch to see if you experience what I am trying to explain.

Julie is a nurse and a friend who accidentally sliced off the tip of her finger as she sat down in a chair at a local restaurant. My wife and I were just about to sit down at the restaurant when Julie sprang to her feet and announced her horror. Without hesitation, I proclaimed, "We're going to the ER," to which Julie commanded, "Not without my finger! Roger, get it!"

I lifted the defective seat, saw the metal frame that had guillotined off her fingertip when she sat down, and eased the flesh off the blade. I placed her fingertip in the palm of my hand, and off we went.

Now I get the heebie-jeebies when I tell that story. That is a physiological reaction. No one died. No one lost a limb. Well, no one lost an entire limb. It was not a near-death experience. But as the reader, perhaps you too had a physiological reaction of deep sympathy with a person you have never met. I want you to watch your physiological reactions closely as you read.[16] Why should you even care for Julie? Why should this story bother you in the least? But you do care, and you are bothered. Does it bother you because it might happen to you? Does it bother you as if it did happen to you or because it could happen to one of your friends or loved ones? Or does it bother you because of some heretofore-unidentified connection we have always had with each other?

I woke from my dream, and my physiology had changed. I was irritated. I was agitated. Even now the memory of my dream invokes within me a physiological reaction. I blush with embarrassment. I warm to the experience. I also feel tired as if the message of my dream has been incompletely interpreted or disseminated, and I have work to do. In that reaction, I recognize that my dream deposited humbling, honest, innocent insight. If the message of my dream is factually correct, then humility is the strongest component of my psycho-physiological response. I am not wise enough to have dreamed up the fact that "I Am You." I am embarrassed to claim the insight as mine, and of course if "I Am You," then this embarrassment is well situated because the insight could not be mine alone. Yet it seems to have come from me but would have to include you. Hot flashes of blushing irritability and agitation accompany this version of affirm, negate, affirm (my idea, not my idea, yet had to be mine). These are the physiological reactions of humbly facing a paradox regarding my smallness in relationship to the immensity of this dream's potential meaning and staggering implications.

I mention the physiological reactions of insight because I am a physician, and I gather stories from my patients regarding their physiological complaints. I have come to recognize how our physiology can deliver information. We can know something, even before our intellect can tell us all that we have just come to know.

I have another physiological reaction when I recall my dream. I experience subtle nausea. I have encountered this faint sensation of nausea often enough to have given it a name. I call it the nausea of adjustment. It is as if I get motion sickness, which I attribute to the rapid acquisition of new information. The nausea of adjustment is a sensation as if changing directions abruptly. You might recall your first trip on an escalator or elevator. It is a subtle sensation. It is in no way disabling. It is easy to ignore or overlook. But it is present and can become nagging. When it disturbs my attention, something significant is knocking at the door of my being.

I also acquired a hat-head sensation. This is not to say that I awoke from my dream with my hair forever matted down about the crown of my head, but I felt as if I had just removed a baseball cap I had been wearing all day. Like the nausea of adjustment, and the nostalgic feeling I will describe, this sensation was intermittent, subtle, in no way annoying, but present and obvious. It curiously came and went, only vaguely connected to the appearance of mysterious events in my life.

My memory of the dream also ushers in nostalgia. I feel an acute homesickness as if I have been taken from a fond place, and I long to return. Or as if I left a place I should have never left and now return to recall my silly decision to leave it in the first place. It is important to be aware of how our physiology responds to insights. New ideas and new awareness might conjure up threatening feelings, goose flesh, a stiff neck, or a clenched jaw. I want you to pay attention to when your chest tightens or when you find yourself uttering a word of disbelief as you read. Your physiology is intelligent. Listen to it. Trust it. Learn to see that understanding often arrives physiologically and before reason can explain what you understand. Try to avoid reflexively extinguishing what you have come to know because you dislike the physical affects it has on you. Threatening feelings might represent on the one hand a threat you should work through, or on the other hand a threat you should work to avoid. A stiff neck might represent resistance to a new idea that you should patiently consider. Your encounter with mystery is more than just confusion. Encounter with mystery is often an encounter with a new insight and exposure to the broader experience of what it feels like being a human.

Haley and My Nausea of Adjustment

I have several anecdotal stories about the nausea of adjustment and its position in the mysticism of the physician-patient relationship. I will offer you one such story about Haley, a swimmer at the University of Notre Dame. Haley had survived a terrible bus accident. The night of the accident, I was called into the emergency room. I learned that she was paralyzed from the waist down. I had no idea how to help. I was not her treating physician. I was only a volunteer with her swim team. I stood at the head of her gurney and whispered to her, "No swelling, no bleeding, no pain."

I quietly explained to her that swelling and bleeding of injuries adjacent to her spinal cord might make her injury worse. I shared with her my belief that we might be able to communicate with our bodies and help their automatic behaviors to be tailored in our best interests. I also told her that if a doctor or nurse told her something that frightened her, then she could suspend her interpretation and bravely ask for clarification. She was to "cancel" her fear and instead be innocently and intensely curious about what she heard and seek out a satisfying explanation.

Haley went off to surgery. She had pressure removed from the spinal cord, but only minimal stabilization was performed because the surgeon did not want to disturb the wounded area with a more massive surgical stabilization. Immediately after surgery, I was in the recovery room, and Haley could move her feet. I got sick to my stomach. I was nauseated with adrenalized awe. It was a very odd reaction. My belly and face quivered with emotional gratitude. It was as if a wave of relief hit me so hard as to induce motion sickness. The evening had been long and arduous, and I suspected my reaction was because I had been bathed in adrenaline all night long. I verified Haley's foot movement with the nurse. We both registered our joy, mixed with reluctance. Haley was struggling to wake up from anesthesia, and we were badgering her repeatedly to wiggle her toes. We wanted to see the proof over and over again. We wanted to make sure her movement was voluntary and not merely a reflexive reaction from a damaged spinal cord. We wanted to make sure she never lost this capacity.

As Haley woke from anesthesia, her body warmed up. The accident had occurred on a cold January night; she had been motionless out in the snow. She was ice cold when she arrived in the emergency department. Then she had been taken to surgery, and now as she warmed up, her movement disappeared. We were frantic! After an acute injury, you often use ice to reduce the swelling and inflammatory reaction. Haley had been resting in snow prior to surgery. We postulated that her wounds must have been swelling as her body warmed up. This edema could cause more injury. Now in the postsurgical period, her loss of function might also represent pressure from a small bleed or clot that was damaging her spinal cord again. We called the neurosurgeon and explained that Haley had moved her feet and now she could not. If this was a window for a miraculous opportunity, what should we be doing? The surgeon listened. He took her back to surgery and inspected her wound. He again relieved any pressure he saw while trying not to add insult to injury. Haley woke from the second surgery still paralyzed from the waist down. I found myself sick to my stomach. It was as if the situation were happening to one of my children, or to me.

Haley's family arrived, and they were amazing. They set out to work on her rehabilitation. They did not look back. They focused on the present moment and how it contributed to the best possible future. Haley and her family would learn to do what they could do with the situation at hand while they would continue to hope for a miracle. My role with Haley had been working on sports-performance imagery and meditation with her swim team. I was an outsider looking in.

I had left her unit early one afternoon several weeks after the accident. I was walking into the physician's parking lot and was hit by a wave of quivering nausea. My stomach and chest shook like they might have if I looked into my rearview mirror to see the flashing lights of a police car. I wondered what had happened to me. What did I eat? How did I get the flu? What had caused this nauseating shiver to course up my belly, into my chest, and across my cheeks and face? Then my pager vibrated. I recognized the number. It was Haley's unit. I turned around and hurriedly returned to the unit. Haley's family was on the phone. There was an urgent commotion in the room. Haley was alert, conscious, and even gleeful. And then I saw it: she was wiggling her toes.

I was nauseated that evening in the surgical recovery room and now nauseated as Haley regained movement in her feet. This was an interesting coincidence. But if coincidences between a patient and a physician happen often enough, one begins to wonder if they are harbingers of the mysticism within the bond of the physician-patient relationship. The two episodes were similar, yet they were clearly different, and still they felt the same. Nausea is not a pleasant physiological reaction. If I were the designer of the signal for how one body might respond to the good news sent to it by another body, I would not have selected nausea. My point is that if "I Am You," then there are things that we know about each other. I am proposing that we might come to know those things through signals that influence our physiology, and this can happen before our intellect decodes the message. If you do not like the feeling, then you might extinguish a valuable message before you are completely sure what is going on. I call it the nausea of adjustment because it takes some getting used to. It is rarely clear if you have mild food poisoning or if you are about to learn something remarkably new.

As for Haley, she returned to the swim team and competed again.[17] The mysticism of the physician-patient relationship is not all cognitive. It has its physiological features as well. Communication within the physician-patient relationship sometimes follows an intuitive less-obvious sequence of events. I cannot prove that the nausea I had in the postoperative recovery room had anything whatsoever to do with the nausea that hit me as I walked into the physicians' parking lot. I cannot explain this apparent clairsentience at all if I-am-not-you. But if "I Am You," then there are things we can know about each other that we delete, distort, or minimize into oblivion because we cannot explain how we know these things about each other if I-am-not-you. We often ignore what we understand because I-am-not-you, and we might not have ignored that same understanding if we believed that "I Am You."

An Intelligence Not of My Own and Physiological Reactions I Did Not Expect

My dream woke me to an intelligence not of my own. I was not allowed to ignore the message of my dream. This mysterious intelligence reached into my life while I was asleep and vulnerable and deposited its unwelcomed idea: "I Am You." It was as if a new computer-operating system was downloaded inside of me as I slept. When I rebooted the morning after the dream, I was upgraded and compelled to think differently. Although I had no time to say good-bye to my former way of thought, the old way of thinking never left me completely. The old way of thinking was transcended and included by this new way of thought. The reality of having access to two ways of thinking can cause confusion and discomfort, which might include this subtle nausea of adjustment. I soon became aware that I felt more discomfort if I tried to ignore the message of my dream. I believe this is spiritual territory.[18] Spirituality does not just influence our minds; it also interacts with our physiology.

After the dream, the idea that "I Am You" became a revelation impossible for me to silence. I could not seem to ignore it. Each time I lapsed into believing that I-am-not-you, I broke a foundational relationship defining our identity, "I Am You." Returning to the belief that I-am-not-you had negative energetic consequences. If I tried to ignore the idea that "I Am You," some physiological aliment would show up to warn me that I could never again hide from this truth. It was as if I awoke with webbed feet. I stumbled every time I tried to run with my former ways of thinking. But I could swim. This dream initiated a new way of thought. Paradoxically, there was something familiar about these heretofore-unimaginable waters. Yet I don't mean to imply that I was an expert at swimming. I still had much to learn.

To my chagrin, I continued to insist upon trying to run because most of my peers ran. It seemed that everything society deemed successful also ran. Thankfully, any physiological disturbance I experienced because I tried to run would promptly dissipate once I agreed to swim—that is, once I began to think, talk, act, or write about the notion that "I Am You." If I ignored this peculiar spirit of evolution that continued to incite thinking that "I Am You," I paid for it with symptoms ranging from mental irritability to a hat head that was never a headache but prompted a lot of head scratching consternation. At times I literally itched to speak up. At other times, my muscles ached with a desire to run with these new ideas. I would get an irritable stomach if I did not work with digesting the "I Am You" food for thought. I had heartaches, shortness of breath, disturbed sleep, and dreams, and I finally figured out that considering the truth that "I Am You" caused all these symptoms to calm down.

I urge you to be aware of these physiological accoutrements to insight. Your physiology might react before complete understanding is acquired. If you catch yourself in the act of reacting physiologically, and you have no idea what is going on, don't automatically assume that you are sick. Stop and listen to your body; something significant might be ready to expand your awareness of your full human nature. But then again, you might just be sick. The road of discovery and insight is not for the timid. The buzzwords for the corporate world include words like "innovative," "entrepreneurial," and "disruptive." The idea that "I Am You" breaks all records for being innovative, entrepreneurial, and disruptive, so be careful what you ask for if you'd like to be on the cutting edge of innovation.

Rapport with Death—Shamus

There are physiological reactions to empathy, rapport, and seeing around blind spots. I have had the feeling of perfect, trusting peace while interviewing patients. It is a feeling similar to what I experienced when I shook hands with myself in the dream. I trust that feeling. It is a reassuring sensation for some patients. But it is disquieting for others. I tread softly as I establish rapport with patients. The physician-patient relationship is privileged and sacred. Your experience of empathy with another person cannot be forced. Oddly enough, some patients do not want honest, empathetic rapport from their physician. Some patients do not welcome seeing around a blind spot. It requires honesty from the patient as well as the physician, and honesty is not easy. "Absolute honesty isn't always the most diplomatic, or the safest form of communication with emotional beings."[19] The following story is an example of how an empathetic exchange did not feel safe for the patient. My sense is that our rapport did not feel safe because the patient could not explain its intensity because he believed I-am-not-you.

Shamus came to see me for acupuncture to address his anxiety. He complained about the stress in the corrosive environment of his academic position. His employer had specific academic demands. In addition, Shamus was being psychologically coerced into fulfilling additional administrative roles. The term "psychological coercion" was the patient's characterization. Shamus was not protected by a tenured professorship.

Shamus had developed a rash whose appearance was an irritant. His red face or neck would betray his emotional state at unpredictable times. His rash was a cosmetic embarrassment. It might appear as a red, blotchy rash crawling up only one side of his neck at a time when he was trying to be firmly authoritative. He felt that his rash jeopardized the credibility of his authority. Shamus also developed an irritable bowel. His stomach might force him out of a meeting at a critical juncture. I am certain there are energetic, organic, psychological, environmental, and genetic factors in his symptoms. I cannot change the genes or the environment. I can attempt to address the energetic, organic, and psychological issues with acupuncture, and that was why Shamus had come to see me.

The first thing I did was to teach Shamus about the connection between his thoughts and his physiology. I explained HeartMath.[20] This is a cognitive technique that has instantaneous physiological effects. You can try a very unsophisticated version of it now as you read. First, think of something that upsets you. What do you feel? I want you to look for a physical feeling not an emotional description. Do you feel tension? If so, then look for the body part that has the tension. Is it your jaw that is clenched, your chest, or your brow? Where is this tension? Do you have a dry mouth, sweaty palms, or tight throat? That is the first part. Think of something that upsets you and then check out your physiological reaction. Is it a deadline? Is it the gossip of a friend, or the overbearing in-law? Now look for how that influences your physiology.

The second part of the experiment is to think of something you deeply appreciate. I would like you to direct your attention to the feelings of deep appreciation and how they your body reacts to appreciation. Perhaps you appreciate the smell of toast, cinnamon, or the smile on someone's face. How do you feel? Again, look for the physiological reaction. Do you smile? Do the muscles in your neck relax? Do you breath more freely? The point is that your thoughts influence your physiology with surprising speed. The HeartMath Institute has pioneered the research of this phenomenon.

I wanted Shamus to see that his physiology responds very promptly to his thoughts. I wanted him to demonstrate to himself that he could modify his thoughts and physiological reactions to stress. I hoped he would see that he could learn a useful skill in a manner of minutes. It was a skill that would help him identify and calm his physiological reaction to an emotional situation. He learned the technique with ease. I printed out the HeartMath webpage. It would continue to serve him well, if he looked into it and then practiced.

Shamus was an adjunct professor of physics. He was also a professed atheist. I didn't have time to ask him about his spirituality or religious inclinations. Shamus proclaimed his atheism with the enthusiasm of an antitheist. He wanted there to be no misunderstanding between us because he was employed by a sophisticated faith-based institution, and he knew from my business card that I was a Catholic physician with a master's degree in divinity. Shamus was equally cheeky about the fact that, as a forty-year-old white male, he was considered a diversity hire at this religious institution because he was an outspoken atheist. We both knew the lie in his joke. Being an atheist at a faith-based institution does not qualify you as a diversity hire, especially if you are a forty-year-old, privileged, Western, white male. His humor was urbane hubris. He claimed that his value to the institution outranked any need to inspect his contribution to the institution's professed religious character, values, or mission. His remark revealed a tension. I understood him perfectly. I did not hold a grievance toward either the institution or the masquerade he was perpetrating. But I would not participate. I did not see the joke. It was not funny to gloat over a breach of integrity with the core values of the institution that hired you.

Shamus was in an institutional culture that said one thing and was doing another. He was a kingpin in the administration of that organization. His health was suffering because he was being asked to go above and beyond as a professor and an administrator. He could not question the oppression of this faith-based employer without invoking a religious value held by that institution toward treating employees with dignity. If he invoked that religious social teaching, he was not sure his charade would survive. The attention he might draw toward himself as an atheist now complaining about being overworked could potentially unseat him. If the institution wanted to remove him because of his resistance to take on additional administrative responsibilities, then his atheistic bent might serve, behind the scenes, as a reason turned to new purposes. He might no longer be the novel diversity hire. "They" might decide that his administrative and academic contributions were not enough to outrank his failure to contribute to the school's faith-based character. He was in a bind. He wanted my help so that he could stomach his duplicity. I was willing to give him that help, but we would not be ignoring the duplicity. I knew his truth. He had told me. I would be just as honest with him as we addressed his health. Would he be honest with himself?

During my intake interview with a patient, I ask many questions. If I get the answer yes to three particular questions in my initial interview, I then ask a fourth question. That fourth question often reveals wonderful stories. But asking and answering that question carries substantial risk because it challenges the norm. I asked the physicist the first question. Was he a perfectionist? Yes. Then he immediately proceeded to define what he meant by a perfectionist, which is what a perfectionist often needs to do because he or she is a perfectionist. In doing so, the patient gives evidence to his or her desire for everything to be in its place.

I asked the physicist the second question. Was he a worrier? Yes. Shamus explained that he has contingency plans, looks down the road, and plans ahead. His description was that of a person taking his perfect conscientiousness to a worrying extreme. Both of these attributes made him a valuable person in any institution. Shamus was conscientious to the extreme and paid attention to detail.

I finally asked him the third question. Was he intuitive? Yes. I then asked how his intuition showed up. He told me he reads situations well. He judges character accurately. He claimed he could easily detect a safe or hostile setting. He could read the direction a meeting was going and figure out how to manage his supporters and his detractors. This was a valuable skill for conflict identification and resolution. I could see that he was a capable, competent, and talented man. His arrogance might be his only threat to job security, but then again it seemed to be a required personality trait at this institution.

He had answered yes to each of the previous three questions. Those three questions acted as a screening tool. This fourth question is always precarious in its own right but less so if I get an affirmative response to the previous three questions. I asked Shamus if he ever had any paranormal experiences. I asked about experiences just bordering on the normal. I asked if he had sensations, premonitions, dreams that came true, or déjà vu. Shamus was a physicist. He was an atheist. He had a mechanical view of the universe. He felt that everything had an explanation and had no respect for the mystical.

However, Shamus quickly answered yes, he had experienced the paranormal. I was delighted. I was surprised he admitted it but then again not surprised, as Shamus did not have a shy ego. He immediately voiced his disclaimer. He felt the paranormal could be explained by science, physics, chemistry, and electromagnetic discharges in the brain, negating the paranormal as actually having anything to do with reality. So, in his opinion, any allegedly paranormal experience was a biochemically creative fantasy. And, of course, if he was right, then he had negated all of what we report of as reality if that report comes from our brains. But I did not argue that point, and he continued to explain his encounter with the world of the fantastic paranormal.

Shamus's leisure pursuits included skydiving and rock climbing. He knew the envelope he worked within, and he knew how far he could push that envelope on each dive and each climb. He knew that just outside the envelope of each jump or climb, there was death. He knew death's escort. He felt the border of death. He experienced the accompaniment of death in every jump and climb. He had much to say about death's character, rules, and allure. He claimed to know death intimately. He knew of death's approach and withdrawal. Death was no different than life if you took consciousness seriously and lived life properly. His explanation was elegant. His insights were provocative and honest. His philosophy was substantial and worthy of serious consideration. His articulation of this unusual experience was poetic and lovely. By my reckoning, his explanation of death's accompaniment during his dives and climbs was a mystical experience of truth. Shamus was an atheist and a scientist. Mysticism was not part of his vocabulary. When his story ended, the room was in the deep, respectful quiet of peaceful, accepting rapport.

Shamus found it off-putting that he admitted this sensation to me within the context of our rapport. He heard himself speaking honestly and then promptly shut down our rapport. I felt him flip the switch. He put the rapport on "force quit." He became polite, cooperatively civil, and aloof. He continued to engage my inquiry, but he shut the door to his complete, honest presentation of self. He was not dishonest, and he answered my questions. But he left himself out. Our conversation from this point forward was between two men with titles and credentials but without souls. He seemed to dislike the fact that he had told me about his experience of death while skydiving and free climbing. In Shamus's story about death, we understood each other. Our rapport was an unplanned loss of between-ness. I understood what was happening, but Shamus did not. Our honest, responsible meeting was the source of his discomfort. In his story, at death's horizon, our first-person points of view merged, and I would go so far as to say they revealed their identical nature. Shamus longed for that merger. He wanted to be understood that well. Shamus respected his characterization of this phenomenon regarding death. He wanted to know that there was nothing between how I understood what he had said and how he understood it. And that happened. As I said, his philosophical thinking and linguistic proficiency defied gravity. I had experienced his truth as if it were my own, because his explanation was riveting. He also wanted to be respected. He wanted to retain mastery over his image. He was not sure he had retained his authority over his truth because he felt the breadth and depth of my reciprocal understanding. Shamus wanted to hold his position of domination over his truth, but truth has no master. Truth is the master.

I understood this physicist's disquieting feeling. I agree that it would have been off-putting if I had this level of intimate reciprocal understanding with someone who I believed was not me. If I-am-not-you, then how could you possibly understand me that well? I-am-not-you is the belief held by almost everyone. Shamus is not the only person who wants desperately to be understood and simultaneously relishes his right to claim that no one understands him. Shamus had to retain his right to be misunderstood. You have a harder time being deceptive if you are clearly understood. You have a harder time shirking responsibility if you cannot claim that you misunderstood or that you were misunderstood. If "I Am You," and we understand each other with better clarity, then it is harder to lie. It is harder to hide. Shamus had come to see me for help living his lie. It wasn't going to work because I was too willing to understand him.

In my dream, as in the physician-patient relationship, I knew I was meeting Me, and that made for a safe, intimate alliance between apparent strangers. I would never do anything to hurt me, and I would never do anything to hurt you. I had no reason to lie to someone who knew me as well as I knew myself in my dream. I had no reason to hide.

With Shamus, I knew that I needed to ease him through the interview because, as a physicist and professed atheist, he only allowed himself to operate as if I-am-not-you. That perspective, I-am-not-you, would not allow and could not explain perfect empathy between physician and patient.

Shamus came to refuse treatment. He said he was a physicist and a scientist, and regardless of the fact that acupuncture has been around for thousands of years, if no one understood how it worked scientifically, then he could not trust the modality. I believe Shamus would not allow for empathy or physician-patient rapport that could not be explained if I-am-not-you. He did not trust himself in a healing relationship that was completely honest. He wanted a relationship with a physician who saw his authority, not one who understood it. His self-designation as an atheist and diversity hire gave him authority outside the realm of his employer's faith-based value system, and he wanted to retain that authority, not have it understood.

If "I Am You," then there is a greater opportunity we will understand each other, and the nature of authority will change. If "I Am You," then domination is a less powerful source of authority. Shamus liked his position of dominance. He feared someone who honestly connected with him well enough to understand his experience with death. A sacrosanct meeting between men is not an easy experience if you insist upon believing that I-am-not-you. Shamus was afraid to get to close to a healing experience in which he was left to manage the wonder of where the healing came from, if it did not come from him or some authority he could explain or control.

Phobias

I would like you to consider the possibility that xenophobia is in some regards similar to the fear generated when Shamus felt understood. Shamus shut down our rapport because he could not explain its intensity if I-am-not-you. Xenophobia is a similar shutdown on a larger and potentially more violent scale. Xenophobia is the intense and often irrational fear mounting into a violent dislike for people from other cultures or countries. The fear and dislike could hardly be justified, because those individuals holding the fears are usually complete strangers to the people they fear. Paradoxically those who fear an unfamiliar group of people and their culture might be reacting to an unexplainable attraction. If, "I Am You," then I might be curious about other aspects of Me that You and your culture represent. If I do not understand the nature of this odd curiosity, then my feeling might be immediately distorted into fear. It is reasonable to become afraid in the face of a spontaneous attraction that seems irrational.

If "I Am You," then part of growing to understand your full human nature might include a desire to explore the full extent of your diversification into other cultures and peoples. A child explores his or her reach, which could be interpreted as exploring the diversity of the body. The child learns that the hand is for grasping, the foot is for bearing weight, and so forth. The child explores balance and walking. A young man explores the full nature of his manhood. An athlete reaches out as far as he or she can reach into athleticism.

We are born into societal prejudices, the most significant being the belief that I-am-not-you. We are born into gender prejudices. Men are not expected to care with the same degree of compassion as woman, and when men do care, we are mislabeled as having explored our feminine nature. Compassion is not a man's feminine nature; it is human nature with a masculine or feminine approach. When women succeed in a "man's world," their success was never a in "man's world"; it was success in a world that excluded women. They extended their reach into a world battling its distorted norms that excluded women. We are curious about who we are and the range of our capabilities, interests, and characteristics. This is true if "I Am You" or I-am-not-you. If "I Am You," then the curiosity about our full human nature includes a natural curiosity toward "other" peoples and cultures. The basic interest you have in the fullness of your nature, while believing I-am-not-you, is now thrust into the larger arena that includes the "other" person. If "I Am You," then you have a naturally occurring interest or curiosity in other people, but you cannot explain your attraction or your interest if you continue to insist that I-am-not-you. When the automatic interest in your full human nature kicks in, and you find yourself attracted to foreign culture, this spontaneous attraction in the absence of an explanation could feel creepy or fearsome and out of your control. Being born with two arms is also out of your control, but it is a norm. Being born with a third arm, or armless, is not the norm and more disturbing. If "I Am You" then it is natural for me to be interested in the apparent "other" person. But, if I am attracted to others and do not understand my curiosity, or we are taught that it is wrong, then our reaction could be to forcefully shut down the attraction.

If "I Am You," then your diversity now includes this "other" person, who is a foreigner. You react defensively when you physiologically and psychologically feel an interest that you cannot account for if I-am-not-you. Society teaches us to fear this attraction toward these strange people and their strange culture because society cannot explain its intensity if I-am-not-you. We have to fabricate arguments, philosophies, ethical and professional codes to overcome prejudicial reactions, because something tells us our prejudices are wrong. I believe the core of that "something" telling us our prejudice is wrong is the fact that "I Am You."

As a man or a woman, if you were attracted to another person of the same sex, and you could not explain that attraction based upon some common ground or obvious connection, then your attraction might feel odd or inappropriate. If I-am-not-you, then you might have been taught that this same-sex attraction is wrong, especially if it drifts beyond certain boundaries. That feeling might be labeled "homophobia" and prompt one set of reactions. If "I Am You," the same attraction might be considered natural and have a different set of boundaries, reactions, and avenues for investigation. I would like you to consider the realm of possibilities that might address xenophobia and homophobia if they were explored from the understanding that "I Am You" is a factor already operating.

Shamus was deeply interested in the rapport that spontaneously established itself. But he could not explain a sense of complete understanding from someone who was a complete stranger by all other criteria. He shut down the rapport because a closeness was felt, which could not be explained if I-am-not-you. Of course there are other explanations. Perhaps he really could not trust acupuncture because science cannot explain how it works. If that is the case, then a large percentage of medications should never be taken, because although science has given us evidence the medications work, science in large part does not completely understand why some medications work. On the other hand, perhaps my arrogance outranked his, and he didn't like losing. Or I was so flagrantly incompetent in my interviewing skills that he feared similar incompetence in my acupuncture needle placement.

CHAPTER 5

If "I Am You," Then What Does This Mean about Time, Intuition, and Peace?

"Peace is the coming together of things that have
never really been separated because 'I Am You,'"
said the experimental subject to the scientist.

The Debriefing Room Within a Dream

My dream was not over when I met myself.

We (scientist and experimental participant) went to an elaborate debriefing room. We verified aspects of what heretofore we would have characterized as our separate lives. We both knew each other completely. This is possible in a dream and should not be a surprise. As the dreamer, I compose of all my dream characters. If I want to, I can design a dream so that I know everything about the characters in it. In my dream, I authentically said, "I Am You." In the design of my dream, the apparent "other" person said to me, "I know." That exchange between dream characters carried the credibility of an exchange between beloved friends. We shared an intimacy and a giving of our selves that was complete, unique, trusted, and knowable, albeit never before had anything like it ever existed as my experience of reality. As the dreamer I authored this exchange. In that composition I created a situation in which I encountered a love I dared not speak for fear of shattering the experience. But in the touch of our handshake, I knew. I knew, as Whyte points out in "Revelations Must Be Terrible,"[21] that I could never hide from this truth again. "I Am You." It was unprecedented rapport, a meeting between two people who seemed more familiar than I am to myself.

The proposal of my dream was the statement "I Am You," which was then married instantly to certainty. My newfound awareness of the truth that "I Am You" was validated in the dream's final sequence of events. In the debriefing room, three questions were put to Me by Me. Although my knowledge was being tested, I already knew I would get the answers right. A fog had lifted. I recognized something about life that I had always known. Yet I knew that I still had much to learn. The truth that "I Am You" was already completely present, and paradoxically more insights were yet to come from Me to Me. I knew that "I Am You" despite all evidence to the contrary. I knew everything about Me, and yet I was about to learn more about what I already knew.

The scientist asked the first question. "If 'I Am You,' then what does this mean about time?"

My response came without a moment's hesitation. I knew the question before it was asked, and I knew the answer with Schopenhauer's sense of self-evident obviousness, which could defy any challenge.

"All time is now, all space is here, and there are levels of parallel existence,"[22] I replied as the experimental subject.

This would mean that the linearity of time is an illusion. Events of the past, present, and future, although experienced in a sequence as if turning the pages in a book, were actually a book finished in the mind of the author. The entirety of that book was capable of instant manifestation, at the speed of light, by mere thought, even if those thoughts changed. This was a book of life capable of accommodating all variations of choice.

We smiled at each other with the gentle relief of trusted recognition. We had both just crossed a boundary. We formerly understood our separation as a barrier between us. We now knew and continued to experience that the separation of our bodies did not represent an impenetrable barrier. If all time and space were now and here, then we were home together as individuals occupying an identical location. This was a place we had always known, and now we lived the proof. Of course all time is now; that is the only way this startling, unrealistic revelation that "I Am You" could bring with it a simultaneous intuition of understanding married instantly with the certainty of intense familiarity. I already knew this place.

The second question was an operational extension of the first.

"If 'I Am You,' and all time is now, then what does that mean about intuition?" asked the scientist.

This question included the intuition of understanding.

"Intuition is then the act of coming to know things and events that have already occurred," answered the experimental subject. There was no magic in looking around a corner and predicting what you will see, if you had already walked around that corner and seen what was there.

A Kingdom Divided and Cancer

This concept is part of my religion's understanding of the Kingdom of God, which is said to be always already present and also something that is in the continuous state of coming. It is an understanding one can bring to the pericope "Peace I leave with you; my peace I give to you. Not as the world gives do I give it to you. Do not let your hearts be troubled or afraid" (John 14:27). There is something we already know about peace and the Kingdom of God that is present and simultaneously yet to come. We are told that the peace of God is already present, and yet it is obviously absent. There is mysticism in the coexistence of these contradictory realities—peace that is simultaneously absent and present. The Kingdom of God has already made its way into human history. The realization that "I Am You" will help us defeat the separations that drive our attempts to extinguish each other in conflicts sanctioned by the belief that I-am-not-you. Peace is the defeat of separation. Peace is looking around the blind spot, which says I-am-not-you, to see that it has always been the case that "I Am You." The final question and answer bring this idea of peace into the forefront.

The last of the scientist's three questions was this: "If 'I Am You,' then what does this mean about peace?"

As the experimental subject, I answered, "Peace is the coming together of things that have never really been separated."

This is how "I Am You" brings us peace: there is no between-ness, and there has been no separation. Conflict requires two opposing forces. "If a kingdom is divided against itself, that kingdom cannot stand. And if a house is divided against itself, that house will not be able to stand" (Mark 3:24–25). Cancer can be defined as a body divided against itself. If the cancerous cells, which are all your cells to begin with, win their fight for individuation and separation from the whole of the body, then the host, which is also you, will die. If there is one thing, if things have never really been separated, then all that remains is peace. This is not a state of homogenization. This togetherness is not something that comes about but something that has always already been. This togetherness lets everything retain its diversity and calls on us all to work out an understanding inclusive of all sides. If "I Am You," then our individuation is transcended and included. We lose nothing. We even retain the delusional experience that I-am-not-you. "You" become my opportunity to experience Me as not me. "You" become my opportunity to experience Me an "other" person. The fact that "I Am You" includes the coming of our realization that we are an expression of the "more to life" that we intuit. We are one person with diverse ideologies, cultures, geopolitical persuasions, and so on. In the dream I experienced knowing and unknowing of all that I previously understood about diversity, division, unity, harmony, and violence. Now, for the first time, I knew peace. "Do not let your hearts be troubled or afraid" was reality. My experience was an acknowledgment that "believing phenomenally less is a necessary, but not sufficient, condition for transcendentally knowing more."[23] I knew less, because that you, which I formerly believed I was not, disappeared. Where there were two, there was now one. I knew the true nature of peace with every fiber of my being because I had experienced letting go of separation. I did not let go. I found that I had let go. It was not my action. There was suddenly no separation. I had been freed from my old attachments to the experience that the "other" person represented someone apart from Me.

The dream ended in a flash of white light as alerting as lightning without the thunder. The flash woke me from the dream. I woke up tormented. I knew something so certainly, yet I feared I would forget it by morning.[24] I quietly scrambled out of bed and snuck downstairs to write down the details of the dream. From the first moment of waking, I was secretive about the dream's revelation. I knew this insight meant trouble in my world. I passionately understood that "I Am You," but outside of the dream state, I no longer felt the peace of this fact with every fiber of my being. "I Am You" was a conviction in the dream, and "I Am You" was not even a concept in my waking world. "I Am You" would be violently opposed in a world invested in the belief that I-am-not-you. I felt exhilarated but alone. But of course there was hope because if "I Am You," then I knew that someone else must know precisely what I knew. My life was haunted by this new awareness. I was plagued by something that everyone should know and no one seemed to know. Perhaps if I had trusted the dream more, then I would not have set out searching for its verification. There is something about searching for validation that can obscure the presence of the truth.

The Story of Rip and the Torment of the Beatific

"Conscience" and "conscientiousness" refer to human attributes that seem to indicate that we know what is right and that there is some sentinel aspect of human awareness that alerts us to right action. We seem to know the full beautiful capacity of human-kind, and yet if we look around we fail to see its regular application. The tension of that awareness tormented one of my chronic-pain patients. Rip experienced a state of being fully alive during his life-threatening accident. He lost the beatific experience of life's fullness during his complete recovery. How is it that complete recovery would lead to torment?

As a nineteen-year-old male, Rip came to see me for chronic pain. He was a fresh-man in college. He drove a small delivery car. One day while on a delivery, he was turning left off of a city street when he was rear ended by a cement mixer. Rip's car was pushed into oncoming traffic, hit head on, and then pushed into a telephone pole that sheared off. In that process, Rip was ejected from his car and ironically thrown onto the front lawn of a local funeral parlor.

Rip had received significant symptomatic relief from his pain through work with his physical and occupational therapists. But there was one aspect of his pain that continued to torture him. Rip was very hesitant to explain. He hemmed and hawed. One day in clinic, he was trying to explain the unique nature of his pain and then stopped abruptly. We were seated across from each other. He scooted his chair closer to me and then leaned forward. Then he stopped again, apparently uncertain about what he was going to say or do. He rested his elbows on his knees and placed his head in his hands as if exhausted and confused. He then raised his head, looked me in the eyes with serious, intense intent, and then reached out and snapped his fingers right in my face as he asked, "Do you know what this is?"

Needless to say, I was startled. A patient just snapped his fingers in my face. Rip did not break eye contact. He was solemn. I was moved. I felt embarrassed. But, for reasons I cannot explain, I did not let my embarrassment dictate what I was going to say. In a flash, I decided to be honest, even if I could not explain my honesty. I did not know where I was going, but I knew something for sure when Rip asked, "Do you know what this is?" I knew. Yes, I honestly knew. But I did not know what I knew. I knew if I said yes, then I had answered truthfully. Yet I might have to prove it to Rip by explain-ing what it was that I knew. But I would cross that bridge when I came to it. At the very moment of his question I knew that my honest answer was yes, and although I was extremely embarrassed to say so and would be more embarrassed if I had to explain, the truth of the matter was that when he snapped his fingers in my face and said, "Do you know what this is?" I knew, and faster than it took for you to read this paragraph, I had answered yes, knowing that I might never survive what came next.

Rip sat up. He exhaled as if he had been holding his breath—as if we were both holding our breath. He knew that I knew that he knew, and that was all. It was a sensation of communion. We were together. He was safe. Our rapport survived, and he began to explain his residual pain.

He said that when his accident happened, he saw in his rearview mirror and felt within himself the horror on the face of the truck driver who hit him. He felt as if he were the driver about to hit him. He instantly felt sorry for that driver. He instantly forgave the driver for his inattention. He knew what it was like to suddenly discover that you were about to plow down a tiny car caught in the path of your gigantic truck. He then saw and felt the fear on the face of the woman he hit head on. He felt her fear as if he were about to hit himself, as if he were she. He was immediately apologizing to her with his eyes. He apologized for being pushed across the median and terrorizing her day. It was as if it was entirely his fault, and yet he knew he was a victim being pushed into that poor woman's fancy car. Rip felt the reactions of both people as if they were simultaneously his reactions. Rip heard and felt the cracking of the paint and bending of the metal of his car. He felt the electricity traveling through the line on the electrical pole he sheared off. He recognized, as if a familiar tune, the song of the bird resting on the electrical line attached to the pole he hit. He felt the bird take flight as his car disturbed the wire the bird was resting upon, as if he were the bird taking flight. He felt the grass grow and the color green beneath his face when he came to rest in the funeral parlor's front lawn. Rip said he had never felt so alive in his entire life. Every second of his accident was suspended in a motionless vat of life's sensory exhilaration. He knew life was "more" than he lived, and during the accident, he disappeared into the "more."

Rip had come to see me for acupuncture. He was looking for the energy to feel alive on a sustained basis. The absence of that fullness of life was torture. He lived as if in a cloud. He interacted with life as if through a fog. The colors, sounds, sights, and sensations of life seemed dull by comparison to the beatific experience he recalled during the accident.

Rip snapped his fingers in my face and asked a question, "Do you know what this is?" His question exposed him to vulnerability. I am not sure he knew what question he was going to ask. But we knew something together, and he knew how to get to the question that would allow him to hear an answer that he trusted. He wanted to know if I would at least try to understand what he was going to try to tell me about the beauty of his pain.

Unlike Shamus, Rip wanted to know that I could understand him with the same intensity as he understood himself. Rip needed to share his wonder, and Shamus wanted to command my understanding of his wonder. When I said yes, Rip trusted that he could tell me everything he knew about his pain. He knew that I knew that he knew. That strange phrase might have an explanation if I-am-not-you. But "he knew that I knew that he knew" is a phrase that requires less of an explanation if "I Am You." If "I Am You," then of course there are things we know about each other. It is not mind reading. It is not invading and acquiring the private details of "another" person's life. But there are things we know. I need your help unpacking the precise nature of this knowing.

Over time, Rip returned to college, was accepted into medical school, and has become a physician. He has no physical pain, and he has engaged life with a wife and one child. Now it is only in the vague recesses of his memory that he recalls the familiar home and fullness of life he experienced during the accident. Getting on with life was mandatory. Life happens to you whether you think you are avoiding it or chasing it. Life is happening to you. Rip does claim that meditation and honest prayer approximated the beatific but do not quite cross the threshold.

My capacity for empathy allowed me to survive the situation of a patient snapping his fingers in my face. We had that safe, sacrosanct alliance and rapport of authentic empathy.

You No Longer Fear the Snakes

Others have described peak life experiences. They say it is as if the lights come on, and those things coiled in the shadows of the mind become illuminated. It is as if you then clearly see the things you feared. Those things are not a nest of snakes hiding out ready to strike you but only a coiled garden hose or harmless rope. When the peak experience is over, the lights go off, and then although you can no longer see the coiled hose or rope, you no longer fear the snakes.

After the dream, I set out to find the proof of what I experienced. If "I Am You," then someone else must know. I did not fear the idea; I feared the process of finding verification. There must be evidence. I wanted conversation. I had my dream before general access was available to the Internet. Library searches were not useful. When I asked for a search for anything on the topic "I Am You" I was asked for clarification. It was not a topic. It had no name. I could only find metaphorical support in poetry or the lyrics of songs. No one had written about my experience. It was not until I could access the Internet that I could cast a broad net searching for someone else who understood that "I Am You." I knew that *if* it was true that "I Am You" then I could not be the only one on the planet to intuit this truth. Like Rip, I longed for the "more" of life. I knew there was that part of me, known as "You" or as those "other" persons, who could contribute to the explanation and validity of my experience in the dream.

CHAPTER 6

A Scholar Admits, Agrees, and Explains the Reality that "I Am You"

Peace I leave with you; my peace I give to you. Not as the world gives
do I give it to you. Do not let your hearts be troubled or afraid.
—JOHN 14:27

If Peace is the Common Ground Why is it so Uncommon?

Have you moved closer to considering the potential reality that "I Am You"? This book is an attempt to coax you into merely considering this potential reality. Jesus promised peace in the Gospel of John. Where is that peace? The world claims it believes in peace. There seems to be a desire for peace. Attainment of peace within the I-am-not-you formula for identity involves massive negotiation and agreement between many separated identities. What if peace is an intrinsic feature of your identity? That would mean that peace is waiting within you. What if the glue to your relationships, the explanation for your attractions, and your longing for a common ground and peace with each "other," is generated by the fact that "I Am You"? If that is true, then perhaps the absence of peace is because of the denial of your intimate connections. The absence of peace is caused by your insistence that I-am-not-you. Peace is already a given reality if you would only stop insisting that I-am-not-you. And this peace was not given as the world gives. This peace is not applied to your situation from the outside. This peace is a given. The fact that you breathe through your lungs is a physiological given. The fact that "I Am You" is a given. This peace is already a part of your identity.

"I Am You," and peace is the coming together of things that have never really been separated. Two parties are required for war, tension, competition, winners or losers, right or wrong, and dissent. Two parties are necessary if I am going to dominate or be dominated. If there is one without a second, then peace comes to us in ways that are more accessible than if we continue to try to prove that I-am-not-you. The fact is that "I Am You" does not eliminate diversity or mandate a sameness that extinguishes individuality. Let me use the characters in my dream as an example of how diversity is preserved. They felt the oneness that still allowed for vastly different and individuated lives because their lives were simultaneously integrated and observed by one dreamer. There is one I-Witness; in that I-Witness exists the home of your identity.

After my dream, I was left with the disquiet of never being able to hide from this fact again. I knew of no one willing to consider the repercussions of the fact that "I Am You." I did not have the person in my life to whom I could come face to face and snap my fingers, asking, "Do you know what 'I Am You' means?"[25] If "I Am You," then why did I suffer the desire to share this fact with You, who are really not "other" than me and ought to already know what I know? If "I Am You," and I lose nothing, then why did I search for what I thought I was missing? "I Am You" felt incomplete without you, or at least I felt incomplete unless I knew that you knew what I knew. But if "I Am You," then you had to know what I knew.

Conviction, Conversion, Course Corrections

This book began with a question: "What if I could convince you that 'I Am You'?" If you have followed what has been said, then you know that is impossible. If it is already true that "I Am You," then conviction is accomplished, and what is needed is a conversion of perspective. I cannot convince you. I cannot convert you. It takes "You" to fill in the gaps and realize the conversion. "I Am You" means that you have joined me in writing this book. I do not, and could not know the entire perfected understanding of this truth. You now need to help make the course corrections necessary for society to safely navigate this awareness. You have to call upon your skills of discernment and help expose the extent of this healing and peaceful reality. My notion is imperfect. I am a reluctant expounder of this truth. It is a terrible revelation because it forces us to the margins of our tolerance and comfort. But if "I Am You," then we are deeply related, and in at least one very significant regard We are identical.

Hazards

I mentioned that You are needed to safely navigate this territory. After my dream, I was afraid. It was immediately obvious to me that the proof that I-am-not-you was violent. I flew beneath the radar. I cautiously searched for someone who could conscientiously challenge this new way of thinking. I wanted to talk this out. I wanted a back-and-forth conversation to discuss the merits of this idea. I wanted to survive learning about the pitfalls, shortcomings, or unanticipated consequences of believing that "I Am You." As I walked around this blind spot there was no guarantee. There was no map. Schopenhauer warned about the path to truth. He said that path moves from ridicule, to violent opposition, and then into the territory of the self-evident obvious. I had been dropped into that obvious territory after my dream. The awareness that "I Am You" was obvious, and in addition it was also only too obvious that ridicule and opposition were still to come.

The many voices in my own head often disagree, so how is sanity negotiated? When you chose to listen to conscience what criteria did you use? Could those criteria serve as a map and outline a safe path around the blind spot that I-am-not-you. The next step might be into a bottomless pit. As I skirted ridicule on the way to meeting those who knew that "I Am You" was obvious, I did not want to meet those who were violently opposed. I did not want to meet the person who would put a gun to my head, shoot me, and then flippantly proclaim, "See? I-am-not-you 'cuz that didn't hurt me," when, in fact, if "I Am You," then we are all affected by the death of another. Perhaps that worry was unfounded and overcompensating. All the same I was cautious and slow to discuss the worldview I was considering.

I need you to help me unpack the concept that "I Am You." I was alone, yet I could not have been alone, and still I felt I was alone, looking for someone who could contribute to a fuller understanding. Even the word "alone" had lost so much meaning. What does "alone" mean if "I Am You"? Feeling alone meant that I knew there was more to life than meets the eye. All the callings in life, from the call of loneliness (which is a call into relationships) to our vocational call, are invitations from the best version of Me to me, and from the best version of You to you. The notion that "I Am You" meant something, and what it meant was not entirely apparent to me alone.

A Croatian American Philosopher and Open Individualism

In January 2012, I discovered the work of Dr. Daniel Kolak, a Croatian American philosopher, and his book *I Am You: The Metaphysical Foundations for Global Ethics.* I found a version of his book on the Internet, and I began to read. I had read only seventeen pages of his six-hundred-page volume when I knew that Dr. Kolak was writing about my experience. I knew I had to purchase his book, because I was stealing from myself if I settled for this copy. Dr. Daniel Kolak's book helped me to understand the odd sequence of events consisting of an intuition of understanding, which comes in advance of reason. He described the truth that we know our ideas are incomplete, and we know our answers are not the only right answers. He reminds us of the threatening feelings we have when the comforts of our ideas are challenged.[26] I had a dream, for gosh sakes. And to my everlasting amazement, comfort, and relief, Dr. Kolak coincidentally used his knowledge of dreams to explain the fact that "I Am You." He wrote an entire book about a meeting with self in a dream.[27] My dream proved nothing. But the experience of my dream was now tormenting my life with its truth. How could I arrive at a truth for which I had never intended to search? I was swimming before I knew what skills were necessary to keep my head above water.[28] In Kolak's book I now had a scholarly sound argument to explain what I understood and why it was such a monumental and humbling insight.

Dr. Kolak had addressed all of this in his book. He explained that understanding does not always follow a sound argument of support. Understanding can reach into our self-deceptions using the same mind that substantiated the self-deception and undo the flaw formerly held by that mind. Dr. Kolak states it this way: "From a phenomenological point of view the intuition of understanding is not something we actively derive using logic and reason from within the content say of particular thoughts but, rather, the intuition of understanding impresses itself upon particular thoughts from *beyond* thought, arriving into consciousness (epi)phenomenally, contiguous with (but not directly caused *by*) the content of our particular thoughts."[29] I knew the truth that "I Am You." Now I set out to examine the presence of that truth in my life. I mentioned earlier that learning how to live on the other side of a blind spot was like walking with webbed feet. I could not walk with my former way of thought without stumbling. I had to swim but still had much to learn. I searched for verification. I wanted to examine the proof and compile the evidence. I found myself considering autoimmune disorders in light of the fact that "I Am You." These are disorders of self, in which self is attacking self. Cancer is self attacking self. Stress-related health issues are often linked to denial of self and the need for rest, leisure, intellectual stimulation, and healthy relationships. Would science look at the illnesses differently if "I Am You"? If we began to think of our identity in terms of the reality that "I Am You," would we look at the destruction of our planet and our ecological blindness as self attacking self by insisting that I-am-not-you?

Dr. Kolak rigorously addressed and experienced the proposal that "I Am You." In his book *The Mysticism of the Golden Rule*, Father Nicholas Ayo comments that Dr. Kolak has done all the "heavy lifting." Kolak exposed the first hurdle to overcome in his preliminary acknowledgments: "The central thesis of *I Am You*—that we are all the same person—is apt to strike many readers as obviously false or even absurd."[30] In that sentence, he revealed the elephant in the room, the dilemma, and the source of the hazards. It was an absurdity to challenge the most fundamental way we understood our selves in the world. Global ethics and the globalization of indifference are both based upon how we have come to treat the apparent "other," operating from the cherished yet mistaken belief that I-am-not-you.

Dr. Kolak coined a term for the experience that "I Am You." He explains that "the traditional, commonsense view of personal identity...[is that] we are each a separately existing person numerically identical to ourselves over time—i.e., that personal identity is closed under our known individuating and identifying borders...[this is the notion that I-am-not-you that Dr. Kolak refers to as] *The Closed View of Personal Identity*, or simply *Closed Individualism*."[31] Dr. Kolak does not prove where our identity resides, but he does offer persuasive exercises to put into question our certainty that I-am-not-you. Dr. Kolak uses philosophy, metaphors, and what he terms "dissolves" to lead his readers to the understanding that if we do not know where our identity resides, then we cannot confidently make the claim that I-am-not-you. He feels that the "*Open View of Personal Identity*, or simply *Open Individualism*...[is] the best explanation of who we are."[32] Open individualism claims that the I-Witness of the life attributed to you and the I-Witness of the life attributed to me are identical.

Where Is God, If "I Am You?"

Dr. Kolak's work is brilliant, erudite, highly researched, densely complex, and will be the gold standard on this topic. Although his sophisticated work discusses the transcendent, he does not place God in the reality that "I Am You." But if "I Am You," then perhaps "I Am" that part of "You" to mind the gap in Dr. Kolak's work and attempt to point at God's place as the voice proclaiming, "I Am You." Father Ayo adds God to Dr. Kolak's "heavy lifting," and I add God to my understanding. But outlining God's place in the fact that "I Am You" exceeds the scope of this introductory volume. God transcends and includes any concept that humankind might conjecture about God, or the excess that is God. My attempt to claim that the big bang is God's utterance that "I Am You" is a claim that will remain one variety of religious experience. It will never be reduced to a text or a proof beyond that found and experienced as canonical scripture.

Dr. Kolak points out that life has been designed so that your experience of the "other" person is convincing. You have been given the freedom to believe that I-am-not-you. It seems to have been the endeavor of the "I Am" to fashion an experience in which "I" had the full opportunity to experience "my" self as something "other" than "me." But the full experience for "other" would also include, in time, coming to know that "I Am" not "other," which is the stage we are discussing, and the experience that "I Am You." Phenomenologically, we experience ourselves as separate individuals, but at the core of our being, at the "I Am," we have the identical I-Witness. We do not know the details of each other's lives, as I seemed to in my dream. If we did know the details of each other's lives, then we would not have an authentic experience of our individual "self" or the "other" person. We cannot read each other's minds, again because that is not an authentic experience of "other." When we come to know that "I Am You," then we expand into a greater sense of self; we do not contract into merely a larger version of me capable of reading the minds of the unsuspecting and apparent "other" person.

There are things that we do know about each other, but we will only come to admit them as we operate from the "I Am You" perspective. Rip snapped his fingers in my face and asked a question I knew I could answer honestly because "I Am You." My answer required nothing more from me than the bravery to say yes. I hesitated for a second but answered out of a place of safety because I knew "I Am You." If I had aborted my honesty, it would have been because I responded out of a place believing I-am-not-you, and because I-am-not-you, then I could not possibly know what the hell Rip was asking. My reaction to Rip was not mind reading, nor was it sharing in Rip's first-person detailed phenomenological life. I was taking a risk when I responded. What we know because "I Am You" will not merely be the summation of what we thought we knew as two apparent "others." It will be more. I suspect borders will remain, outlining our individual nature—just as a finger is not a hand, but they are both body, or an iceberg is not the ocean, but they are both water. But I do not believe the borders of our individuality are impenetrable barriers separating us from the identical nature expressed by the fact that "I Am You."

Mom Is on Her Deathbed and Still Rescues Chrissy

When my mother was dying, I spent the last several days with her in our home. One night I sat in a recliner chair at her bedside, and my wife, Chrissy, slept on the floor at the foot of her bed. I lay awake watching Mom. My father and sisters were sleeping in the other rooms of the house. I was gazing out into our backyard as the snow fell past the lights under the eaves outside the window. I wondered how Mom's last breath would appear and how I was going to handle her death. It was the middle of the night, and Mom, who had been rather quiet for the past day, abruptly sat up in bed, looked down on the floor at my sleeping wife, and said, "Chrissy, Chrissy, your breathing!" Mom was shouting at Chrissy. Mom was directing Chrissy to be aware of how she, Chrissy, was breathing. Then Mom quietly lay back down in bed. I had noticed nothing about Chrissy's breathing, but I rocketed forward in my chair to listen to my wife. I was watching my mother, waiting for her next breath and was completely inattentive to my wife. Chrissy was peacefully asleep, her breathing restful and calm. She did not seem to have stirred with Mom's startled warning.

The next morning, Chrissy asked me if Mom had said something about her breathing during the night. I was surprised to learn that Chrissy had heard anything at all. She had seemed to be asleep. I told her what Mom had said. Chrissy explain that she had been dreaming. Two of her friends were browbeating her about some trivial event, and as the dream proceeded, she had become upset and began to hyperventilate. Chrissy never has panic attacks in her waking life, but in this dream, she was frantic to explain her situation to these women and find relief from their verbal attacks and cattiness. In her dream, as Chrissy began to hyperventilate, she heard Mom's voice firmly draw attention to the fact that she was dreaming and could calm down. It was as if Mom had access to the events of Chrissy's dream. Or, at the very least, the border that seemed to separate Mom and Chrissy seemed more permeable than one might expect. Mom knew something about Chrissy, and Chrissy heard Mom. This incident can probably be explained if I-am-not-you, but there is another explanation if "I Am You." If "I Am You," then Mom and Chrissy are connected and they do know things about each other.

Mom died in February 2000. I still speak to her. I do not miss her—well, yes, of course I do, but then again I can honestly say I do not miss her because she always feels present to me. I dream about her. I get advice from her. Now this sort of relationship with my mother as my closest deceased ancestor might not deviate from how you, my reader, might interact with your deceased family and friends. But if "I Am You," and we have an identical I-Witness, then that I-Witness has in some way existed before we were born and continues after we die. This might be an explanation for humanity's cultural inclination to maintain and value relationships with ancestors.

How, then, might what we know because "I Am You" show up? It might show up in how we relate to our deceased ancestors. It might show up as our humanitarian gestures. It might show up in the hope that seems to come out of nowhere when you are in a hopeless situation. "I Am You" as an experience might show up like it did with Emily, Gia, Margaret, Shamus, and Rip. It will involve risks and walking into territory based upon an intuition of understanding that will only be verified after you have taken some steps along that walk. "I Am You" is a present reality, and the mysticism in the physician-patient relationship is just one example of how that experience shows up.

Social Implications and Hope

You should now be able to see that this countercultural position that "I Am You" holds significant questions and hazards. If "I Am You," then where is the evidence, and what is the nature of the authority by which we dominate each other? If "I Am You," then what does this mean about society's winners and losers, property rights, possessions, right and wrong, or the true nature of self-interest, greed, empathy, jealousy, envy, compassion, collaboration, altruism, generosity, and solidarity? If "I Am You," then who is the perpetrator of evil, and who is responsible for sexual assault, child abuse, pedophilia, or murder? What does this mean about the unborn, sin, or death?

If "I Am You," and there is no "other," then who told me that "I Am You"? Look at this last question again. If "I Am You," and there is no "other" person, then who is left to have told me that "I Am You"? Who manufactured my dream? Who identified my blind spot and offered me this story in order to see around the blind spot known as the belief that I-am-not-you? What is the nature of this mystical intelligence that reached into my life and deposited this idea in a dream? It was my dream, so the intelligence was mine. Yet it was an intelligence that was not mine because I had never known this idea as part of my reality. It was a blind spot. A blind spot by definition is something you cannot see. Yet the intelligence exposing this vacancy in my understanding had to be mine because the insight came from me. I can explain this dilemma if "I Am You" because then it was that part of Me that is You that helped me see around the blind spot. I cannot explain how I saw around a blind spot without an outside influence if I-am-not-you. Yet I recall no such outside influence. If you are the source of this outside influence, and you never presented this idea to me, then how could I have received this information from you? The idea that "I Am You" must have come out of thin air. And perhaps the idea did come out of thin air. The point is that I cannot as easily explain how I knew what I did not know, if I-am-not-you. Yet I must have known, because the idea came to me in a dream manufactured by me.

The standard norm for identity is that I-am-not-you. I-am-not-you is our enculturated escape clause. It is the mythological meme adopted by humanity across the globe, which frees us from any culpability in the suffering of "others" not directly in our path. I-am-not-you, so I can cheat you, abort you, starve you, steal your natural resources, oppress you, pollute your stream, confiscate your property, or chose not to cooperate with you, or you can die, and it does not need to affect me.

As your physician, I-am-not-you, so when your situation of pain or suffering haunts my sleep, this must mean I am weak because I have failed to maintain my professional distance from you. When your suffering affects me, it must be because I am too involved or because my physician-patient relationship has lost its professional edge. If I-am-not-you, then when I continue to care for you in the face of your insults, your lack of compliance, or your outright lies, it is because my professional code mandates that behavior. I have an intuition of understanding that questions the claim that what happens to you does not need to affect me. That intuition of understanding tells me that many of the generic conclusions we arrive at because we believe that I-am-not-you are wrong. I do not continue to care for you merely because of a professional code. I care. I care because "I Am You," and we are intimately related.

If "I Am You," then whose illness is my patient's? If "I Am You," does this mean the trials of my life come from Me toward Me? There are answers for these questions, and they require your input.

The most devastating and fearsome implication is this: To what extreme will the apparent "other" person go in order to avoid and silence the responsibility inherent in a proposition that claims "I Am You"? Authorities have their systems of control. Who is the ultimate authority if "I Am You"? How does an authority maintain its power if there is no "other" person? Authority will be redefined if "I Am You." The redefining of authority will be interpreted as a threat to those who continue to believe I-am-not-you. The domination systems of the world will go to warring extremes to prove I-am-not-you, and in that process they are cancerously destroying themselves. Yet if "I Am You," then We have access to a new understanding of this self-destruction. If "I Am You," then We have to develop a new understanding of our self-interests.

There are things we know about each "other" if "I Am You." If "I Am You," I would not dominate, oppress, or subjugate you. I would try to help you and hope for you. Hope often seems to appear in convincingly hopeless situations, and perhaps that hope came from you. We already know that starvation, war, spoiling your environment, cheating you, aborting you, failing to collaborate with you, pedophilia, murder, sin, rape, poverty, the illness of the "other" person, and the starvation of a stranger do affect us, and we know this profoundly. Knowledge of the profound effect atrocities have upon us is the origin of our hope. Our social and environmental illnesses cannot be addressed unless we first know they represent suffering and are wrong. We know these atrocities are wrong. How do we know? Why do we know? Who is this singular I-Witness that knows that "I Am You" and informs us that in oppressing "others" we are hurting ourselves? Where is the evidence supporting this profound intuition of understanding that murdering you cannot lead to peace? Why have we been granted the freedom to believe that I-am-not-you? In what way does the world change if "I Am You"? What things remain familiar or perhaps become even more familiar if "I Am You"? Those answers rest with Us.

Alone, I cannot convince you of this reality; that requires a conversion of thought inclusive of You and every sentient being. This territory is now Ours to explore. You are not alone. We can treat each other better than we do. We can give and receive better than we do. The belief that "I Am You" might give you the bravery and confidence needed to treat the apparent "other" person with more kindness and attention.

Do you recognize that if "I Am You," then it was "You" who called me to write this book? "You" accompanied me in writing it. It is my hope that with God as our guide and through our personal exploration of the mysticism of love of neighbor,[33] and specifically through examples I offer from the mysticism of the physician-patient relationship, then we can set out to explore the magnitude of our human dignity with the understanding that "I Am You." I hope you have now arrived at a place where you feel safe to tinker with the suggestion that "I Am You" and that as you do so, you will find more health and peace—because we always already knew that we are all in this together.

Epilogue: Attractions between Strangers and Dear Friends Because "I Am You"[34]

met a wonderful seventy-five-year-old Notre Dame alumnus en route to his reunion weekend. My wife and I were returning to our home near Notre Dame. We were awaiting our flight from Albuquerque to Chicago.

I am an introvert. I was minding my own business reading a book in the airport. A complete stranger sat down next to me and enthusiastically interrupted my reading. He wanted to alert me to the fact that he was a fellow Notre Dame alumnus.

Honestly, I did not welcome his invasion, albeit he was a gentleman to the most exemplary degree. Spontaneous intrusions startle me. I am more reserved. I did not deserve his attention. I did not ask for his attention. I did not know what he expected from me. I did not understand his attention. I was not obligated to give him my attention just because he wanted to talk. But I knew the right thing to do, and I accepted his barging in with calm politeness belying my internal kerfuffle.

This man had walked by several times. I felt his attraction. I felt my withdrawal. He had stared at my Notre Dame ring. I slid it behind my book. It is not easy for me to converse with a stranger. He then gazed at the ND insignia on my sweater. The logo was a bit more obvious. Why did I bother to wear that trademark if I did not want to draw attention to my university affiliation? The simple emblem had accomplished its declaration and attracted attention. It was my own fault. It's like purple hair; if you don't want people to stare, then why make it purple? What would this stranger expect from me? I had felt his initial hesitation, and I endorsed his reluctant nature. But the extroverted youth of this genial older man had jumped the walls of his hesitation. I felt all of this.

How is it that we can detect the inquiring gaze of a stranger? How do we feel the attention from others or our attraction to others? If I-am-not-you, then there must be some pheromone or magnetism that science has yet to detect. Or was all this merely truth in advertising, and that branded interlocking ND was completely responsible? Or, if "I Am You," then something in our identical nature was sending us forth to investigate our broader existence. He and I were going to learn about our broader nature. What ingredient in the fingerprint of a stranger's attention allows it to leave smudges that penetrate the glass case enclosing our individuality and then lure us into conversation? How are personas defined? How is it that personas are even perceived?

The phenomenon of detecting an attempt at rapport before it has actually been established can be a creepy feeling. Part of the peculiar nature of the probing gaze from another person is the fact we are not quite sure if it is real or imagined. We can all discern a gaze. We can register someone's curiosity. But we can lie to each other about the intentional or unintentional character of our gaze. You know when a department store salesperson is heading your way. You know the salesperson you might enjoy dealing with and the person who rubs you the wrong way. When you are talking to someone on the phone, you cannot even see him or her, and yet you know when he or she has stopped paying attention. How do we know? These phenomenon could be explained if I-am-not-you. I think these incidents of heightened awareness are more easily explained if "I Am You." My point is that these experiences might seem unnerving and even provoke fears or phobias. If "I Am You," then we know something about each other, and we are not absolutely sure how we came to know it or why we might feel an affiliation or an attraction. When you feel an attraction toward someone or attention is given to you by someone, and you cannot explain your feeling of inquiry or explain why you might be the target of another's inspecting gaze or curiosity, then fear can step in as a reflexive protective response. I did not know what this man expected. I did not like it. But I did get over it.

Sam introduced himself. Then my wife and I met his wife. They told us about their family, and we reciprocated. They planned on taking a bus from Chicago to Notre Dame. We invited them to ride with us. During the drive Sam repeatedly told me how excited he was to be seeing his dear friend at the reunion. Sam and his wife were both thrilled about the trip back to the university to see their dear friend.

I was intrigued by Sam's repeated use of the phrase "dear friend." I really wanted to know what this wise older gentleman meant when he referred to someone as a dear friend. I was not sure if I could ask him about this characterization. I cast caution to the winds and I asked him what made for a "dear friend." I have to emphasize how unsure I was about taking my conversational privileges to this personal extreme. Our conversation had only been superficial chatter up to that point. We were still strangers. I felt intrusive. Sam's executive demeanor merited respect. But I ventured into his private territory. At first Sam's response was a friendly diversionary ho-hum, and he waived off my inquiry as if I should know what he meant. I pressed his CEO exterior for a bit more honesty. Why was he a dear friend? Sam said that as dear friends, they attended the weddings of each other's children, made contact on holidays, joined each other at the funerals of mutual friends, and had traveled together with their wives to many exotic places.

That explanation should have been enough, but apparently it was not because I continued to inquire. I told Sam that his explanation certainly clarified why he was a friend, but I persisted. Sam's expression "dear friend" had captivated my attention, and I wondered if it meant more, or was it merely an expression that had fallen into disuse by subsequent generations? I liked his expression. I hoped I was qualified to be someone's dear friend. I wanted to understand.

Sam then explained that this man was a survivor of a most terrible World War II ordeal. It was for that reason that this friend was Sam's lifelong role model for survivorship. I agreed. That clearly defined a very good friend. I injected some of my own sentiments regarding my good friends, but I stubbornly continued to wonder what qualified this man as a "dear" friend.

I had just met Sam. At this point, I was actually rather put off by my own pushiness. I was sure I had a no right to ask for a more intimate understanding. Sam turned quiet after my third inquiry, and I felt he might remain silent for the rest of the trip. I seemed to be called to ask these questions—but then, of course, I wasn't called—still it seemed as if Sam had somehow instigated my inquest by his constant referral to this man as a dear friend. In the silent gap between my third inquiry for a deeper explanation and Sam's reply, I had just enough time to begin doubting my motives for asking about Sam's "dear friend" designation.

Then Sam spoke. He almost blurted out that he loved this man. He was attracted to him. Sam loved just being in his company. They did not even have to speak. They took great pleasure from sitting in the same room, being in the same car, or falling asleep on the same patio waiting for the sun to set. Their emotional friendship was tight. He held high his bond with this man. It eclipsed other bonds he had with other men. They deeply respected, appreciated, longed for, and enjoyed each other's company, the lives they had lived, and the families they had built.

I asked Sam if he ever told this man that he loved him. My goodness gracious, I was amazed at my audacity. It was as if I knew Sam had great wisdom to share, and I would not let up until I understood. I also felt that Sam needed me to learn that he loved this man. I oddly felt that my impertinence had been summoned to be of service to both Sam and me. Sam said his friend just knew that he loved him, and that was all that was needed. I then asked Sam, if he were visiting this man at his deathbed, would he then tell him that he loved him? Before I could yell at myself, "What the heck, Klauer, do you want this man to throw you out of your own car?" Sam thundered out, "Certainly! And I'm not afraid to tell him that when I see him."

I had walked out on this limb, and Sam was gracious enough to allow me access to the reasoning behind his definition of a "dear friend." We had survived the fruits of our inexplicable attractions. We rested in the quiet of our new wisdom, refreshed and friendly. Then the conversation resumed with an honest reflection upon his "dear friend" designation and the odd nature of my interrogation. The ride flew by in congenial deep conversation. Our parting handshake communicated reverent mutual esteem.

How is it that I knew I could do this when, in fact, I did not know, yet surely I did know? I am not that pushy. I am not that self-assured interviewing a stranger outside the confidential structure of my medical office. How is it that Sam knew that his friend knew that they loved each other, when those words had never been exchanged? These are the things we know about each other that can be explained if I-am-not-you, but I find easier to explain if "I Am You." I knew that Sam knew that I knew what this "dear friend" designation meant. But I did not know this without the input from Sam's part in our conversation. If we understand the meaning behind the fact that "I Am You," then a phrase like "I know that he knows that I know" is a phrase exposing an epistemological pathway that is arduous to explain if I-am-not-you but lends itself to a more direct explanation if "I Am You." If "I Am You," then we know when we are called to ask questions, and we know when we are drawn toward people without an obvious explanation for that attraction. We know when we have been granted a privilege, but we also know we must politely exercise that privilege.

Sam's dear friend was his role model for survivorship. As for survivorship, I think that if we are going to survive as a species, then we, especially men, will have to pay attention to whom we are attracted and assume nothing. I was poised to rebuff Sam's attention, but conscience directed my polite response. Sam might have been ready to push me out of my car, but he thundered out his declaration of love for his dear friend. As men, we are going to have to learn to express our genuine appreciation for each other and deal with the accountability that accompanies love. All of humankind can make improvements in how we express reciprocal appreciation.

I think homophobia is polite fiction for our cowardice and at times our total failure as men to learn a variety of ways to investigate or express simple attractions or deep love for each other. As men, we have to do the work to figure out how to handle our attractions and find the courage to express our genuine friendly affection. In some cases, like Sam and his dear friend, we should express our love for each other. I wonder if homophobia is fueled by the belief that I-am-not-you. I believe that homophobia and xenophobia would have a more difficult time existing if we came to understand that "I Am You."

We have championed our infatuation with individuality and taken it to a lonely, unhealthy, and warring extreme. Showing men that they are our dear friends should not fall into the category of missed opportunities recognized on our deathbeds. We could end up self-destructing as a species unless we admit that there is a range of healthy and loving same-sex attractions, and we can find our place on that spectrum. Perhaps the twenty-first century terms man crush and bromance have come into existence to explain the expanding prevalence of what was once known by the twentieth century expression dear friend.

As men, we need to learn how to express affection for each other, which I feel Jesus might have had with the apostles, and they might have had with each other. I think Christ very likely had a dear friendship and cherished relationship with Saint John, the beloved apostle, and Mary of Magdala. We should admit our deep caring for each other and develop healthy social skills and enough stamina of character to admit and explore same-sex attractions. This is only one of the hurdles we will have to overcome as we come to understand that "I Am You."

If I was walking on the road to Emmaus (Luke 24:13–35), I imagine my first attraction to Christ would be a deep, intimate feeling. Would I allow myself to invite Christ to dine with me, as they did in that biblical story, or would I be too homophobic? There is a risk in that invitation, and our fear is not unfounded. But we must discern whether this is a fear we must recognize and investigate or a fear we should legitimately run from and avoid.

If "I Am You," then there are things we already know about each other. We might explain those things using a term like "dear friend." We might experience those things as an impulse to pry into a total stranger's definition of a dear friend. Sam and I survived our prying. Sam pried into my quiet reading, and I pried into his private friendship. Sam knew something about his safety as I probed, and I knew something about Sam's willingness to express his love. As a result, we learned more about the depth of our human dignity and breadth of our human existence.

As I quoted in the introduction, "All truth passes through three stages. First, it is ridiculed. Second, it is violently opposed. Third, it is accepted as being self-evident"

(Arthur Schopenhauer, German philosopher, 1788–1860). I hope you have passed the stages of ridicule and violent opposition and have come to a place where it is at least a bit more obvious that "I Am You." We are deeply related. If "I Am You," then we have far-reaching, radically sweeping, personal reasons to be at peace, reasons that are urgently in our self-interest. If you are now willing to consider the possibility that "I Am You," then you will see that your life holds within it the author of its ongoing course in miracles.

END NOTES

1. Daniel Kolak, *I Am You: The Metaphysical Foundations for Global Ethics* (Dordrecth: Springer, 2004), 380–81.

2. "Always already" is a two-word phrase that seems redundant. In his book *The Eye of Spirit: An integral Vision for a World Gone Slightly Mad* (Boston, Shambala Publications, 1997), Ken Wilber uses this term. The title of the twelfth chapter in that book is "Always Already." I use the term to indicate the timelessness of what I am referring to when I say "always already." I also use the phrase to indicate that there are things in place that we might not have admitted as real but come to see that we have somehow known them to be present all along. For example, there is no need to search for the truth about our identity because the truth has always already been given to us. The search implies the absence of something that is present but not fully recognized. We need to honestly look at our situation and come to see. I want to give Ken Wilber credit for introducing me to the phenomenon of this two-word expression. I will use it frequently, and "always already" is not a redundancy but an experience.

3. Phenomenological or qualitative research might be more lenient in this regard. That research method might take anecdotal evidence and look for trends. This book does not claim to be that scientific. I merely want to persuade you to consider a new way of thought and see if it brings you closer to a sense of health and peace.

4. Haley Scott DeMaria and Bob Schaller, *What Though the Odds: Haley Scott's Journey of Faith and Triumph* (United States: Cross Training Publishing, 2008).

5. "I-Witness" refers to the identity that witnesses the life script that is attributed to you. ID is the abbreviation for identity or identity documents. The I-Witness is the first-person point of view in front of which the life attributed to you passes. The I-Witness is that thing that claims the life attributed to you. That part of you that claims, "This is mine" or "This is me" is the part of you that we are calling your I-Witness or your identity. The events of your interior life (your interior self-talk or conversations with yourself, thoughts, secret motives or desires, values, judgments, critiques, and all mental or intellectual activity) are witnessed by your

I-Witness. These events of your interior life pass in front of this I-Witness. The events or script of your exterior life also pass in front of a viewer or that part of you that sees your life, its contents, contexts, ups and downs, and its claimant. This is your I-Witness.

6.   Daniel Kolak, *I AM YOU*, xxii.

7.   Ibid, xxii.

8.   Father Nicholas Ayo, CSC, introduced me to the terminology "mysticism of love of neighbor" as he juxtaposed it to the sense of the mysticism of love of God. See his book *The Mysticism of the Golden Rule* (Notre Dame, Indiana: Corby Press, 2016).

9.   David Whyte, "Revelation Must Be Terrible," DavidWhyte.com, Many Rivers Company, accessed April 30, 2014, <www.davidwhyte.com/english_rev.html>. This poem was originally published in David Whyte, *Fire in the Earth* (Many Rivers Press: n.p., 1992).

10. I will capitalize "Me" when I am referring to a version of me that is the best version of me. I experienced the reality that there is a Me inside of me that is the best version of me, and I will capitalize that version as Me. You know who you would be at your best. We are not often successful at being our best, but we have some idea what that would look like. I am referring to that Me.

11. David Whyte, "Revelation Must Be Terrible."

12. Keep in mind that I am expanding the definition of Me. I am exposing a reality that we have many divergent voices in us and many ways you can represent your singular self as many selves to the world. When you place our best foot forward that is coming from the capitalized "Me."

13. Capitalized "Me" again implies there is something "more" to this "Me" that we can experience, and we can admit that this "more" exists slightly beyond that represented by just "me," although it is not separated from me. It is my contention that part of this "more" that is Me comes from You.

14. Daniel Kolak, *In Search of Myself: Life, Death, and Personal Identity* (Belmont: Wadsworth Publishing Company, 1999), 173.

15. Helen Riess and Chriss Gordon, "The Formulation as a Collaborative Conversation," *Harvard Review Psychiatry* 13, no. 2 (2005): 112.

16. If you do care, then perhaps that is why you checked out this endnote. I care for you, too, and I can't leave you without the happy ending. Julie's fingertip survived the trip to the ER and was reattached, and all is well. She had a period of paresthesias (odd feelings in the fingertip), which has near-complete resolution, and she is typing again with an occasional zinger to remind her of the incident. Her recovery was impaired primarily by the reaction of the restaurant owner, who insisted that the seven of us who witnessed this event were lying. He tried to block his insurance company from covering the medical expenses. Happily, the medical expenses, Julie's legal expenses, and a bit more were covered.

17. Haley Scott DeMaria and Bob Schaller, *What Though the Odds*.

18. The words "spirituality" and "mysticism" declare a specific territory. I believe that God is active in our lives and in everything. I use the words "spiritual" and "mysticism" to expose the realm where words begin to fail, yet the experiences the words attempt to apprehend are real experiences. If what is said in this book is truth, it is a truth that has always been present. If what is written here is truth, then what is said here is a prophetic clarification and not prophetic in a predictive way but in a revelatory way. I am reluctant to claim a role in any revelation. And if "I Am You," then you had a role in this clarification too. Still it seems that I am the one coerced to ask you to consider this concept of identity. My reluctance chafed against the force urging me to write. That chafing had a physiological reaction, and it might be of psychological origins, but I have come to consider the origins to be spiritual.

19. Jonathan Nolan, Christopher Nolan, *Interstellar*, directed by Christopher Nolan, Paramount Pictures, Warner Bros., Legendary Pictures, Syncopy, Lynda Obst Productions, 2014. A quote from TARS, a robot in the 2014 movie *Interstellar*.

20. "HeartMath," HeartMath, Inc., (April 29,1016), <http://www.HeartMath.com.>

21. David Whyte, "Revelation Must Be Terrible."

22. This would mean that past, present, and future all exist right now. I came to understand this as if I always understood this; it was as if the truth of its expression manifested itself. If I once believed all time was now, I did not recall it, yet there now seemed to be no time in the past when I could not recall believing that past, present, and future were in one place (the now), and our physiology, brain, body, and reasoning could come to understand and experience this truth. I wonder if consciousness traveling at the speed of light is the now.

23. Daniel Kolak, *I Am You*, 392.

24. As you can see, "Do not let your hearts be troubled," was not my surviving sentiment upon waking from the dream. The invasion of my worry was my spiritual mistake. I failed to trust "You." Thinking that I would forget the dream might have been a valid concern, but how do you forget reality? The scope of this book does not allow for further discussion of this intricate detail of the life of mysticism. I will only comment that I did not give myself this insight, and nothing I could do, not even writing this book, was going to hold onto this insight. It was a given. It could as easily be taken away.

25. Chrissy takes issue with this comment. She was aware of this new idea. She did understand. She was not driven to find others who understood. She did not understand my burning requirement for a conversation. When she read this passage she said I could have snapped my fingers in front of her and she would have known.

26. Daniel Kolak and Raymond Martin, *Wisdom without Answers: A Brief Introduction to Philosophy Fourth Edition* (Belmont: Wadsworth Publishing Company, 1999), 2.

27. Daniel Kolak, *In Search of Myself.*

28. The experience of knowing a little about a monumental insight is intimidating, frightening, and hazardous to explore. I now find myself contacting CreateSpace to set into a published format the extent of my inadequate understanding of the fact that "I Am You." This is what I mean by swimming before I have the skills

to keep my head above water. Father Nicholas Ayo is an accomplished writer. He has ventured into this territory in his book *The Mysticism of the Golden Rule* (Notre Dame, Indiana: Corby Press, 2016), and TortoisWind has taken a crack at getting her head above water in her book, *I AM YOU:I AM YOU* (United States: TortoisWind, 2015). These books are evidence that the experience known to us as the expression, "I Am You," is showing a more prominent profile. My experience does not match that of Father Ayo, who allows for I Am you, and I am not you. My experience fits only in title and passion the reports of TortoisWind's work. She contends that I am you and you are me, which is not my experience nor the experience outlined in my book. Fr. Nicholas, TortoisWind, and I do find a place for God in our experience. Daniel Kolak's body of work is still the groundbreaking gold standard.

29. Ibid., 380–81.

30. Ibid., xiii.

31. Ibid., xxii.

32. Ibid., xxii.

33. The "mysticism of love of neighbor" was a phrase introduced to me in spiritual direction by my director, Father Nicholas Ayo, CSC. His comment was that the mysticism of love of God had led most mystics to a notion not unlike the experience of Saint Paul, who claimed that he no longer lived, but it was Christ within him that lived. Father Nicholas and I were conjecturing about what form the experience of the mysticism of love of neighbor might take. Father Nicholas coined the phrase in our conversations. See his book *The Mysticism of the Golden Rule*. (See also note 5.)

34. Roger G. Klauer, MD, 1975, "The Love That Dare Not Speak Its Name," React Online, *Notre Dame Magazine*, Autumn 2004, http://magazine.nd.edu/news/10626-the-love-that-dare-not-speak-its-name-p-1/, accessed April 29, 2016.

33101310R00056

Made in the USA
Middletown, DE
30 June 2016